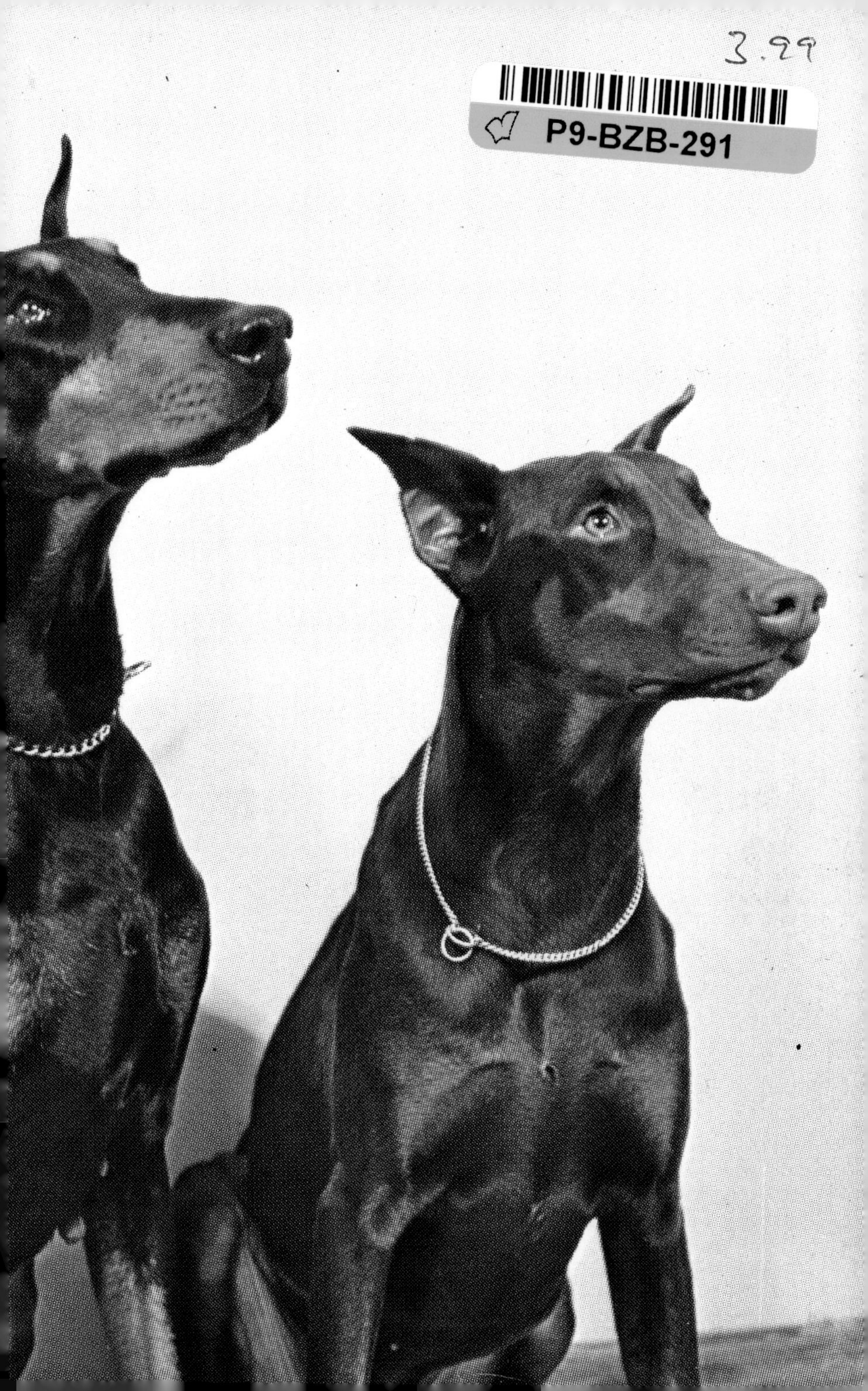

CONTENTS

FRONT COVER: Ch. Marwood Anubis de Scudamore and Reikon of Stocklea, owned by Mrs. Janet M. Skidmore, Scudamore Dobermans, Norwalk, Connecticut.

Most photos in this book taken by Louise van der Meid, except those by Vince Serbin, pages 7, 11, 12, 14, 15, lower 22, 32, 33, 46, 47, 114, 115, 118, 119, 122, 123.

Mr. Serbin's pictures possible through the cooperation of Von Arian Kennels, owner, Olivia Soriano, Howell, New Jersey.

KW-009
ISBN 0-87666-698-5

© 1979 by T.F.H. Publications, Inc., Ltd.

Distributed in the U.S. by T.F.H. Publications, Inc., 211 West Sylvania Avenue, P.O. Box 427, Neptune, N.J. 07753; in England by T.F.H. (Gt. Britain) Ltd., 13 Nutley Lane, Reigate, Surrey; in Canada to the book store and library trade by Beaverbooks, 953 Dillingham Road, Pickering, Ontario L1W 1Z7; in Canada to the pet trade by Rolf C. Hagen Ltd., 3225 Sartelon Street, Montreal 382, Quebec; in Southeast Asia by Y.W. Ong, 9 Lorong 36 Geylang, Singapore 14; in Australia and the South Pacific by Pet Imports Pty. Ltd., P.O. Box 149, Brookvale 2100, N.S.W., Australia; in South Africa by Valiant Publishers (Pty.) Ltd., P.O. Box 78236, Sandton City, 2146, South Africa; Published by T.F.H. Publications, Inc., Ltd., The British Crown Colony of Hong Kong.

DOBERMAN PINSCHERS

by KERRY DONNELLY

1) and 2) show good representatives of dog show winners. 3) A close up of placement of support bar. 4) Close up of young Dobe's ears after cropping and taping have been completed. 5) A mature Dobe with uncropped ears. While American Doberman Pinschers are rarely seen with uncropped ears, this is not the case in all countries in which the dogs are popular.

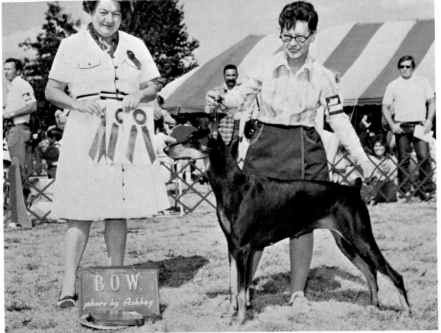

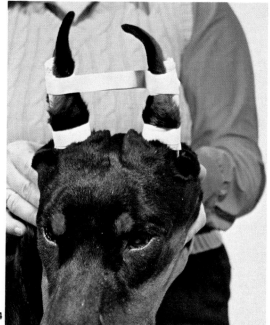
3
4
5

The Doberman Pinscher was developed in Germany for use specifically as a guard dog. The founder of the initial strain of Doberman envisioned his ideal dog as powerful without great bulk, and possessing great stamina and intelligence.

1. HISTORY OF THE BREED

The Doberman Pinscher has come a remarkably long way in a relatively short time, having skyrocketed to the height of popularity with both the dog show fancy and the general public. The breed can trace its origins back only as far as the 1880s, thereby classifying it as one of the most modern of the working breed. The namesake of the Doberman is Herr Louis Dobermann, a local magistrate from the town of Apolda, the state of Thuringia, Germany. He is credited with having founded the initial strain, which classifies the Doberman Pinscher as a "man-made" breed. Among Herr Dobermann's many duties was tax and rent collection, and caring for the local dog pound. He came upon the idea of using the stock he had at his disposal to breed the perfect guard dog that would serve to protect him on these collection rounds of the town. All the while knowing that this "ideal" guard dog would have to be powerfully built and remarkably strong, Dobermann itemized what he would require by way of character traits and began selecting dogs to be his base stock. His initial attempts at inbreeding the local dogs centered on producing litters of black, large sized, alert dogs that were neither shy nor overly aggressive. Obedience was the prime character trait.

Common to that southern area of Germany in 1884 was the German Pinscher, a dog that was far from handsome, but was unmatched in fearlessness and ferocity. These dogs came to be the base stock that was chosen to be the progenitor of today's Doberman Pinscher. Herr Dobermann selected various even tempered dogs of the appropriate conformation (most likely German Shepherding dogs, unlike the German Shepherd Dog of today) as crosses to modify the sharp tendencies of the Pinscher. Since Herr Dobermann owned and much admired the Rottweiler breed, he bred some of his finest specimens to the emerging "Dobermann's Dog," as they were known locally, to add the additional size and massiveness. Other purebred breeds that are assumed to have figured in the early crossings are, naturally, the dogs found in Germany in great numbers at that time: Great Danes, German Shorthaired Pointers, Weimaraners (from which the genes for blue coloring are credited), Setters, Dachshunds, and the Black-and-Tan Terrier, now known as the Manchester Terrier. Many theories also trace the Doberman ancestry to the Beauceron or "Red Sock", a French shepherding dog that had markings very similar to those of modern Dobermans.

Herr Dobermann always kept in mind what his "ideal" dog would look like. He had to be a sleek black dog of unending stamina, strength and intelligence. Although the initial bone structure of the Doberman was

1) The less frequently seen blue coat is apparent in this head study of a mature Dobe. 2) The desired attentiveness of the breed is caught by the healthy female Dobermans here and in 3). 4) The cat's lack of fear at the proximity of this sleek black Dobe belie the belief that Dobermans are fierce by nature. 5) On black Dobes, as the one on the right, black nose and dark eyes are preferable according to the standard. In the reds, a brown nose and lighter eyes are accepted.

4

5

1) In large kennels concrete floors in outside runs are a matter of practicality, for daily clean-up is required to maintain a suitable level of sanitation. 2) Kennel design showing a line-up of runs; each run shares a common partition though dogs in each run are completely separated from each other. 3) For a change in exercise pattern, a small number of dogs share a large outdoor pen that is unattached to the main shelter.

1

2

3

quickly arrived at, the desired short sleek coat presented problems, since most of his stock had long, wiry or wavy hair. The smooth-coated Manchester Terrier is credited for the standardizing of the coat, and for passing on its black and tan coloring and markings. The Manchester breed standard requires a "thumb mark" patch on the legs and "pencil marks" lines running on top of each toe; although these particular markings are undesirable in today's Doberman, many puppies are still born with such markings, which disappear within several weeks of birth.

As generation after generation of "Dobermann's Dogs" were produced, their popularity with the town folk rapidly increased, as good-sized alert watchdogs were always at a premium. Through the years the breed name changed in its homeland from Dobermann's Dogs, to Thuringer Pinschers, Plizelich Soldatenhunds, and finally Doberman Pinscher. As the type slowly became fixed, and the breed began to spread throughout Germany, other breeds took up the task of bringing these early specimens to a point of fine stylization. Most notable among these was Otto Goeller, one of the very earliest breeders, who also came from the town of Apolda. He is credited as being chief architect and sponsor of the breed, and he did much to stabilize the qualities of the early dogs.

In 1899, five years after the death of Louis Dobermann, Otto Goeller organized the National Doberman Pinscher Club, headquartered in Apolda. The first actions of the club were to write the first official standard for the breed, and to finalize the breed name. In recognition of his work in developing the breed, the name of Doberman Pinscher was officially adopted to honor Louis Dobermann. In 1900 the German Commission of Delegates, the controlling organization for dog fanciers, officially recognized the breed as being purebred. Since the black and tan dogs were breeding true to type, this color was recognized as being desirable, while all others were disqualifying. A year later after intense study of the color coding patterns within the breed, recognition was also granted to the blue and tan and the red and tan Dobermans.

In the early 1900s breeders concentrated on refining the coarse, thick bodies and heads that were being produced, traits which undoubtedly traced back to the early Rottweiler influence. Steady progress was made in their homeland until the onset of World War I and the famine of 1916, which all but destroyed not only the Doberman Pinscher but nearly all dogs (and people) alive in Germany at the time. The first exportations of Dobermans to the United States had taken place in 1908, and the early stock was flourishing in its new homeland. As the famine continued in Germany, and malnutrition set in, concerned breeders opted to sell their finest specimens to American fanciers rather than have them die or be killed for food. Among these exports was Lux v d Blakenburg, one of the

1

2

1) The ear cropping operation takes place when the young Dobe is between 2 and 3 months old. After the ears have been cut by a veterinarian, a bar is placed on the center inside ear to hold it erect. 2) Tape is wrapped around the ear and supporting bar to hold the latter in place. 3) The ears are taped together to ensure they grow upright. 4) A cropped ear with the supporting bar taped in place and before it has been taped to the other ear.

3

4

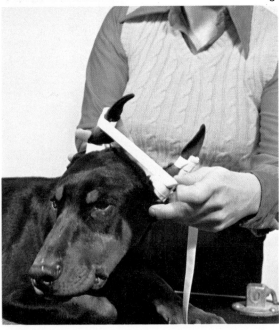

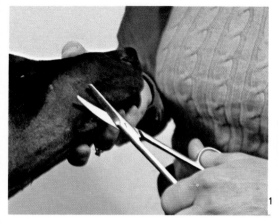

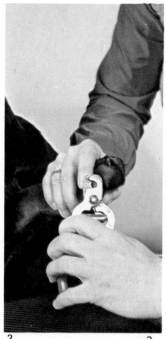

1) Trimming the whiskers of any breed is necessary only if your dog is a show dog. 2) Special clippers are available for clipping your dog's nails. 3) All the grooming tools, coat conditioners and shampoos necessary for keeping your dog looking his best are usually available at your local pet store.

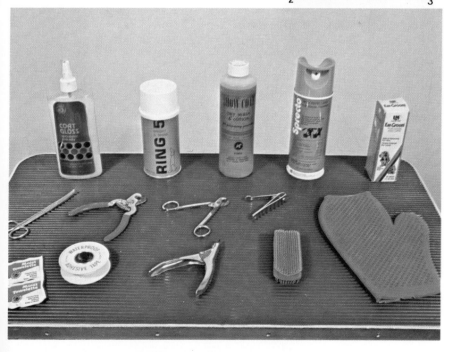

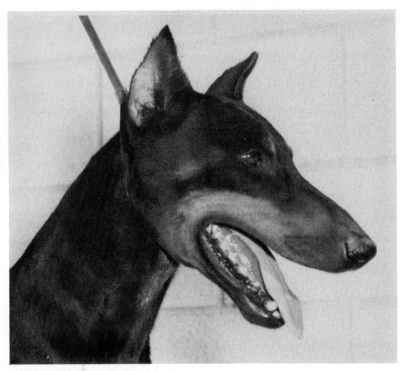

The modern Dobe's head is sleek, resembling a wedge that reaches its broadest width at the base of the ears. This present structure represents a refinement of the early 19th century Dobe that still reflected much of the coarseness and bulk of the earlier Rottweiler influence.

greatest sires of all time in his homeland, who went on to have a great influence on the course of the breed in the U.S. In the succeeding years in Germany the breed was once again brought to a state of stability and refinement, and through the far-seeing efforts of those early breeders that placed their stock in safe homes, little of the heritage of the German Doberman Pinschers was lost.

In the last half decade, a uniform elegance has replaced the coarseness of the early Doberman Pinscher specimens; however, through it all the instinctively alert, loyal and watchful temperament of the breed has held true. The original breed standard drawn up by Otto Goeller and the National Doberman Pinscher Club in 1899, although revised in some minor points of conformation, has remained basically the same over the years. It is one of the most exacting and precise of all standards, and has served well in fulfilling Herr Louis Dobermann's dream for the "ideal" dog.

1) Earlier ancestors of this Weimaraner puppy may have contributed to the coloring of our modern Doberman Pinscher. Weimaraners were one of the several breeds that were crossed to develop the Doberman breed in Germany and were used specifically to contribute their genes for blue coloring. 2) A Dobe stands beside a piece of equipment used in obedience training.

1 2

Ranking among the most popular breeds of dogs in recent years, Dobermans, well known for their prowess in obedience competition, present an impressive appearance in conformation rings as well. But modern breeders, guided by the national breed club, continually strive not to breed out the original guard dog characteristics in favor of conformational considerations.

2. DOBERMAN PINSCHER BREED STANDARD

In its homeland of Germany in 1899, the National Doberman Pinscher Club drew up the first standard of perfection for the breed. This standard was adopted by all countries recognizing the breed, and was used in the United States from 1908, when the breed was officially recognized, through 1935 when the Doberman Pinscher Club of America submitted a slightly revised version to serve as the new American standard. Included in this chapter is the original standard devised in Germany, followed directly by the American standard. Through many generations of breeding and modifying of the Doberman Pinscher, it was inevitable that the original standard would need to be modernized to incorporate the adjustments that had been made within the breed. The original standard serves as the guide for the ideal working Doberman, while today's standard lays the boundaries for both working and show dogs.

Appearing here will be the most recent Doberman Pinscher standard, revised as of 1969. The 1935 version was amended in 1948 to include adjustments in size and head, as well as to point out that these dogs should be fearless and aggressive, but not shy or vicious. The 1948 standard was again revised in 1969, this time to emphasize the importance of having the proper tooth count. It was agreed that any Doberman with four or more missing teeth would be disqualified from show competition. These changes are aimed at retaining guard dog characteristics, which might have become secondary in importance if breeders were allowed to highly stylize or streamline the breed for the show ring. Allowing conformational points to take precedence over original purpose has often had deteriorating effects on many breeds. The Doberman Pinscher Club of America, and all its supporters, are determined to keep their breed as close to the original "ideal" as possible.

THE GERMAN STANDARD, 1899

GENERAL APPEARANCE: The Doberman Pinscher should be built muscular and powerful, but not clumsy and massy; neither should he be greyhound-like. His appearance must indicate swiftness, power and endurance. Temperament should be lively and ardent. *Height* at the shoulder: Males 21.6 to 25.6 inches; females, 18.9 to 21.6 inches. *Length* from occiput to first joint of tail about 27.5 inches.

TAIL: Cropped, not longer than 5.9 inches.

HEAD: Top of head must be flat or may be slightly arched, but the forehead must be broad; stretched long, the head must go over into a not too pointy muzzle. *Cheeks* must be flat but very muscular. A dog of about 19.7 inches in height at the shoulder should measure about 16 inches around the forehead. The length of the head, from occiput to the tip of the nose should be 9.9 to 10 inches.

BITE: Must be very powerful, well developed and closing right. Lips lying close to the jaw, not drooping.

EYES: Must be dark brown, medium sized, with an intelligent, gentle but energetic expression.

EARS: Cropped, not too short, not too pointy.

THE AMERICAN STANDARD, 1969

General Conformation and Appearance: The appearance is that of a dog of medium size, with a body that is square; the height, measured vertically from the ground to the highest point of the withers, equalling the length measured horizontally from the forechest to the rear projection of the upper thigh.

Height: at the withers—**Dogs:** 26 to 28 inches, ideal about 27½ inches; **Bitches:** 24 to 26 inches, ideal about 25½ inches. Length of head, neck and legs in proportion to length and depth of body. Compactly built, muscular and powerful, for great endurance and speed. Elegant in appearance, of proud carriage, reflecting great nobility and temperament. Energetic, watchful, determined, alert, fearless, loyal and obedient.

The judge shall dismiss from the ring any shy or vicious Doberman.

Shyness: A dog shall be judged fundamentally shy if, refusing to stand for examination, it shrinks away from the judge; if it fears an approach from the rear; if it shies at sudden and unusual noises to a marked degree.

Viciousness: A dog that attacks or attempts to attack either the judge or its handler, is definitely vicious. An aggressive or belligerent attitude towards other dogs shall not be deemed viciousness.

Head: Long and dry, resembling a blunt wedge in both frontal and profile views. When seen from the front, the head widens gradually toward the base of the ears in a practically unbroken line. Top of skull flat, turning with slight stop to bridge of muzzle, with muzzle line extending parallel to top line of skull. Cheeks flat and muscular. Lips lying close to jaws. Jaws full and powerful, well filled under the eyes.

Eyes: Almond shaped, moderately deep set, with vigorous, energetic expression. Iris, of uniform color, ranging from medium to darkest brown in black dogs; in reds, blues, and fawns the color of the iris blends

Graham

A fine American specimen of today's modern Doberman, reflecting the current American standard for the breed. Today's dog ideally incorporates the characteristics called for in the original German standard aimed at keeping it a working dog bred for specific types of work. It also takes into account latter day provisions of both German and American standards which incorporate points necessary for conformation show excellence.

1

2

1) This trio of Dobe puppies exhibits the well-defined markings above eyes, on muzzle, chest, and legs, allowed in the standard. The pups will soon be of an age appropriate for cropping the ears. 2) These young Dobes are being trained for police work to assist lawmen in a New Jersey municipality.

with that of the markings, the darkest shade being preferable in every case.

Teeth: Strongly developed and white. Lower incisors upright and touching inside of upper incisors—a true scissors bite. *42 correctly placed teeth,* 22 in the lower, 20 in the upper jaw. Distemper teeth shall not be penalized. **Disqualifying Faults:** Overshot more than three-sixteenths of an inch. Undershot more than one-eighth of an inch. Four or more missing teeth.

Ears: Normally cropped and carried erect. The upper attachment of the ear, when held erect, is on a level with the top of the skull.

Neck: Proudly carried, well muscled and dry. Well arched, with nape of neck widening gradually toward body. Length of neck proportioned to body and head.

Body: Back short, firm, of sufficient width, and muscular at the loins, extending in a straight line from withers to the *slightly* rounded croup. **Withers:** pronounced and forming the highest point of the body. **Brisket:** reaching deep to the elbow. **Chest:** broad with forechest well defined. **Ribs:** well sprung from the spine, but flattened in lower end to permit elbow clearance. **Belly:** well tucked up, extending in a curved line from the brisket. **Loins:** wide and muscled. **Hips:** broad and in proportion to body, breadth of hips being approximately equal to breadth of body at rib cage and shoulders.

Tail: Docked at approximately second joint, appears to be a continuation of the spine, and is carried only slightly above the horizontal when the dog is alert.

Forequarters: Shoulder Blade: sloping forward and downward at a 45-degree angle to the ground meets the upper arm at an angle of 90 degrees. Height from elbow to withers approximately equals height from ground to elbow. **Legs:** seen from front and side, perfectly straight and parallel to each other from elbow to pastern; muscled and sinewy, with heavy bone. In normal pose and when gaiting, the elbows lie close to the brisket. **Pasterns:** firm and almost perpendicular to the ground. **Feet:** well arched, compact, and catlike, turning neither in nor out. Dewclaws may be removed.

Hindquarters: The angulation of the hindquarters balances that of the forequarters. **Hip Bone:** falls away from spinal column at an angle of about 30 degrees, producing a slightly rounded, well-filled-out croup. **Upper Shanks:** at right angles to the hip bones, are long, wide, and well muscled on both sides of thigh, with clearly defined stifles. Upper and lower shanks are of equal length. While the dog is at rest, hock to heel is perpendicular to the ground. Viewed from the rear, the legs are straight, parallel to each other, and wide enough apart to fit in with a properly built body. **Cat Feet:** as on front legs, turning neither in nor out. Dewclaws, if any, are generally removed.

Gait: Free, balanced, and vigorous, with good reach in the forequarters and good driving power in the hindquarters. When trotting, there is strong rear-action drive. Each rear leg moves in line with the foreleg on the same side. Rear and front legs are thrown neither in nor out. Back remains strong and firm. When moving at a fast trot, a properly built dog will single-track.

Coat, Color, Markings: **Coat,** smooth-haired, short, hard, thick and close lying. Invisible gray undercoat on neck permissible. **Allowed Colors:** Black, red, blue, and fawn (Isabella). **Markings:** Rust, sharply defined, appearing above each eye and on muzzle, throat and forechest,

An intense alertness and aggressive manner characterize the typical Doberman attitude. However, viciousness or hairtrigger temper should not be mistaken for these former desirable traits. A dog exhibiting the latter traits in the show ring will be immediately disqualified.

American Dobermans are preferred with cropped ears; the breed in many other countries is normally shown with drop ears.

on all legs and feet, and below tail. **Nose:** Solid black on black dogs, dark brown on red ones, dark gray on blue ones, dark tan on fawns. White patch on chest, not exceeding ½ square inch, permissible.

FAULTS

The foregoing description is that of the ideal Doberman Pinscher. Any deviation from the above described dog must be penalized to the extent of the deviation.

DISQUALIFICATIONS

Overshot more than three-sixteenths of an inch; undershot more than one-eighth of an inch. Four or more missing teeth.

APPROVED OCTOBER 14, 1969

Like certain other breeds of large working dogs that have been bred for guard duty, the Doberman has often been maligned for his ferocity. Untrained, he responds with warmth and affection to those who treat him with kindness. Once trained, it is wise to teach him beyond any doubt whom he must protect.

3. BREED TEMPERAMENT AND CHARACTERISTICS

The Doberman Pinscher is a working dog by heritage, designed to perform the tasks of guard work and sentry duty, and to serve as loyal companion in the home. While many negative words have been spoken about the alleged ferocity of the breed, these rumors have had no adverse effect on its popularity, as the Doberman Pinscher ranks with the German Shepherd Dog and Poodle as the most popular of all purebred dogs. As protectors of the home they are unequalled, both as natural deterrents to crime and for subduing any unlucky intruders that should happen to make the mistake of testing their abilities.

To succeed in the tasks for which Dobermans have been bred, certain tendencies are of prime importance to their temperament. Fearlessness and aggressiveness are essential. To complement and enhance the value of these tendencies, the intelligence and retentiveness of the breed comes into play. Perhaps the Doberman Pinscher's finest character traits are his unquestioning obedience and loyalty to his master. Without these latter qualities, the aggressiveness of the breed might go unchecked giving rise to dogs that are the fearsome, vicious animals that many uninformed people believe the breed to be.

While very early specimens of the breed were reputed to have "hair trigger" tempers, concerned American fanciers have consciously bred out these undesirable traits without decreasing the natural coverage and strength. Over the decades since the arrival of the first import, much progress has been made. Today's well bred Doberman is not prone to violent outbursts, although unstable dogs from poor breeding stock can be found in this and every breed. With the skyrocketing popularity of the breed in recent years, a disproportionate demand for Doberman puppies has been created. If left unchecked, unscrupulous, uncaring or uninformed breeders out to supply this demand can do great harm and set back the progress knowledgeable breeders have attained in stabilizing and enhancing the breed. It must be stressed that instability is more a sign of poor breeding than it is a breed characteristic, so potential puppy buyers should determine the quality of the parent stock and its probable effect on the health and temperament of their puppies before ever purchasing one. Eliminating the market for "mass produced" dogs will go a long way in maintaining the quality of this and every purebred breed.

By nature the Doberman is a peaceful dog. Left alone, he goes his own way. Only when he is attacked or asked to defend his charge does the instinctive, potential ferocity come into play. He is naturally protective of

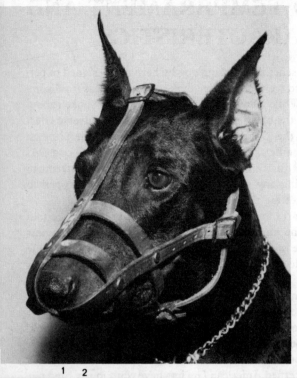

Muzzles are rarely a necessity in dogs that have been taught whom they are to guard and whom they are to guard against. In the trained guard dog that is also kept for a pet and companion this is an important distinction. 2) Many dogs that are to be trained for police work spend most of their time between pen and trainer. It is not unusual that the only personal attention they receive is from their trainer and the police partner they work with while on duty.

1   2

Two Doberman puppies portray the characteristic inquisitiveness the breed is known for. Though at this young age they still may have the privilege of lolling about in a pastoral setting, the future may hold a demanding role for them, calling upon every trait of physical strength, mental keenness and aggressiveness to fulfill it.

those he loves and will make use of all his keen senses in his chosen role as protector. What most people who call the Doberman a violent, ferocious dog fail to consider is that the properly trained Doberman works strictly on the orders of his master. Although there are natural abilities present, the Doberman Pinscher does not come complete with the knowledge of how to attack and defend; it is a learning process for the dog in which he makes use of the instincts that have been bred into him.

Even the most ardent supporters of the breed will agree that the Doberman Pinscher is not for everyone. While rumors that Dobermans are nasty and dangerous by nature are exaggerated, there still is an aggressive instinct in the breed that must be channelled properly. In order to do this, an owner must be willing to give adequate time to obedience training his dog. Without this, the intelligent, retentive nature of the dog will not be

Even as a puppy, the Doberman exhibits an alertness and readiness for whatever is to come. His energy is boundless and as he matures he will remain a desirable companion if all of his enthusiasm is consistently channeled into the type of behavior his owners consider acceptable.

A Doberman that is well bred, selected carefully at the time of purchase, and treated with affection and kindness makes a doubly desirable pet, combining strong protective tendencies with his usual needs for companionship.

allowed to reach its potential, and this is a misuse of a dog that has been bred to serve. Dobermans, like children, must be properly trained so that they can understand what is expected of them. Like all dogs, the Doberman Pinscher should be owned only by a family in which he will really fit. The temperament of the dog and his physical requirements cannot be too far removed from the potentials of his surroundings.

The character of the Doberman can be quickly summed up by the terms alert and eager. They require a large amount of daily exercise, for they border on being high-strung if kept inactive for long. A Doberman is not given to barking without provocation, and his bark is a warning to be heeded. While he is not a bully, he will not back down from any or all that confront him. Since they are brainy and strong willed, they should be trained from an early age to the rules of the household and treated affectionately. With those he loves he will sport an almost clownish temperament, but around strangers he is naturally aloof, suspicious and standoffish. Given proper introductions he will accept anyone he is told to; however, he will make it a point to sleep with one eye open as long as there is a stranger in the house!

1) A Dobe puppy wearing an ear rack begins basic obedience training. 2) Team of mature Dobes that have attained advanced obedience training. 3) Even the well-trained guard dog enjoys an occasional snooze on the couch. 4) The same pup as pictured in 1) gets a lesson in the "sit" command from the trainer's youngster. 5) Even a fully grown adult dog may not have completely outgrown his chewing needs. He should be quickly and firmly reprimanded to prevent such a temporary lapse of manners from becoming a habit.

4   5

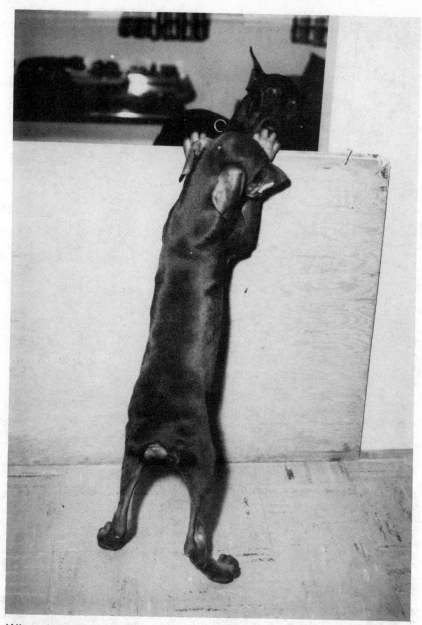

When the new Dobe puppy enters your home for the first time, it is wise to confine him to one room of the house where he does not have ready access to perishable belongings and where it is convenient to begin housebreaking him.

4. THE DOBERMAN PUPPY

PREPARING FOR THE PUPPY'S ARRIVAL

In choosing a puppy, be certain beforehand that each member of the family is truly enthusiastic about having this particular breed of dog as an addition to their circle. Dogs are much too intelligent not to sense whether or not they are liked. If your puppy feels unwanted, you may find an unhappy dog on your hands that could easily turn into a "problem child." Before buying, research the breed and make sure it is the one for you. Besides reading, a good way to learn about your prospective pet is to observe one of the same breed in its permanent home surroundings. Most owners will be only too happy to show off their furry friend.

One of the most important factors to consider when selecting a dog, whether it is to be a pet or show dog, is its temperament. When looking at a litter of puppies for a prospective purchase, spend time just quietly observing them. Usually the most outgoing or aggressive puppy is your best bet. However, do not overlook the more reserved puppy. Most dogs are wary of strangers, so reserve may indicate caution, not timidity. He may calmly accept your presence when he senses that all is well. In any event, never force yourself on a puppy—let him come to you. Beware of the puppy that hides in the corner and won't emerge until you have left. Chances are he will always be high-strung and may develop more undesirable habits as a result of his nervousness.

Because at least three out of four prospective purchasers of dogs want to buy a young rather than an adult or almost adult dog, the problem of preparing for the arrival of a permanent canine house guest almost always means preparing for the arrival of a puppy. This is not to say that there is anything wrong with purchasing an adult dog; on the contrary, such a purchase has definite advantages in that it often allows freedom from housebreaking chores and rigorous feeding schedules, and these are a definite benefit to prospective purchasers who have little time to spare. Since the great majority of dog buyers, however, prefer to watch their pet grow from sprawlingly playful puppyhood to dignified maturity, buying a dog, practically speaking, means buying a puppy. Before you get a puppy be sure that you are willing to take the responsibility of training him and caring for his physical needs. His early training is most important, as an adult dog that is a well-behaved member of the family is the end product of your early training. Remember that your new puppy knows only a life of romping with his littermates and the security of being with his

1   2

1) Dobe pups should be able to handle a diet of completely solid food by the time they are eight weeks old. If the litter is large, using more than one feeding dish will insure every pup getting its fair share.2) Dobe pup on left has had his ears cropped, wrapped and taped to remain erect. Puppy on right still retains the drop ear the Dobe is born with. 3) Young Dobe being weighed in. Checking your puppy's weight regularly is one sure method of guarding its good health. 4) A Doberman mother enjoys a fresh air outing with two of her offspring.

3   4

mother, and that coming into your home is a new and sometimes frightening experience for him. He will adjust quickly if you are patient with him and show him what you expect of him. If there are small children in the family be sure that they do not abuse him or play roughly with him. A puppy plays hard, but he also requires frequent periods of rest. Before he comes, decide where he is to sleep and where he is to eat. If your puppy does not have a collar, find out the size he requires and buy an inexpensive one, as he will soon outgrow it. Have the proper grooming equipment on hand. Consult the person from whom you bought the puppy as to the proper food for your puppy, and learn the feeding time and amount that he eats a day. Buy him some toys—usually the breeder will give you some particular toy or toys which he has cherished as a puppy to add to his new ones and to make him less homesick. Get everything you need from your pet shop before you bring the puppy home.

MALE OR FEMALE?

Before buying your puppy you should have made a decision as to whether you want a male or female. Unless you want to breed your pet and raise a litter of puppies, your preference as to the sex of your puppy

When it is time to select a puppy, you should have decided beyond a doubt, beforehand, that the Doberman is the breed for you. Acquaint yourself with it through books and other Dobe owners. Then look for a puppy that is alert, clear eyed, and of sound structure.

If you are looking mainly for a pet, whether your puppy is male or female is not very significant, except that a female left unaltered will have to be watched closely when she comes into heat.

is strictly a personal choice. On the whole both sexes are pretty much the same in disposition and character, and both make equally good pets.

SHOW DOG OR PET?

It is well to define in your own mind the purpose for which you want a dog, and to convey this to the breeder. A great deal of disappointment and dissatisfaction can be avoided by a meeting of the minds between seller and buyer.

Although every well-bred healthy member of the breed makes an ideal companion and pet, actual pet stock is usually the least expensive of the purebred registered stock. The person who asks for a pet, pays a pet-geared price for the animal. Pet stock is least expensive because these dogs are deemed unsuitable for breeding or exhibition in comparison to the standard of perfection for the breed. Generally only skilled breeders and judges can point out the structural differences between a pet and show quality dog.

If you are planning to show your dog, make this clear to the breeder and he will aid you in selecting the best possible specimen of the breed. A show quality dog may be more expensive than one meant for a pet, but it will be able to stand up to show ring competition.

WHERE TO BUY YOUR PUPPY

Once you have decided on the particular breed that you want for your pet, your task is to find that one special dog from among several outlets. Buying a well-bred, healthy dog is your foremost concern. By doing a little research in the various dog magazines and newspapers you can locate the names and addresses of breeders and kennels in your area that are known for breeding quality animals. The American Kennel Club will also furnish you with addresses of people to contact that are knowledgeable about your chosen breed.

Your local pet shop, although necessarily restricted from carrying all breeds in stock, may sometimes be able to supply quality puppies on demand. Due to the exorbitant amount of space and time needed to properly rear puppies, pet shops generally prefer to assist owners by supplying all the tools and equipment needed in the raising and training of the puppies. The pet shop proprietor, if unable to obtain a dog for you, can often refer you to a reputable kennel with which he has done business before.

SIGNS OF GOOD HEALTH

Picking out a healthy, attractive little fellow to join the family circle is a different matter from picking a show dog: it is also a great deal less complicated. Often the puppy will pick you. If he does, and it is mutual admiration at first sight, he is the best puppy for you. Trust your eyes and hands to tell if the puppy is sound in body and temperament. Ears and eyes should not have suspicious discharges. Legs should have strong bones; bodies should have solid muscles. Coats should be clean. Lift the hair to see that the skin is free of scales and parasites.

Reliable breeders and pet shops will urge you to take your puppy to the veterinarian of your choice to have the puppy's health checked, and will allow you at least two days to have it done. It should be clearly understood whether rejection by a veterinarian for health reasons means that you have the choice of another puppy from that litter or that you get your money back. Be sure to get the details of this policy before you purchase any puppy.

PAPERS

When you buy a purebred dog you should receive his American Kennel Club registration certificate (or an application form to fill out), a pedigree and a health certificate made out by the breeder's veterinarian. The registration certificate is the official A.K.C. paper. If the puppy was named and registered by his breeder you will want to complete the transfer and send it, with the appropriate fee, to the American Kennel Club. They will transfer the dog to your ownership in their records and

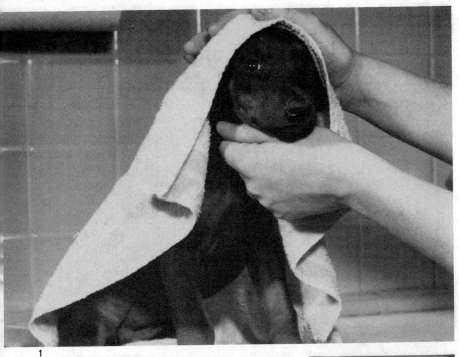

1

1) Most puppies have not had a chance to become dirty enough to require a bath. But if unusual circumstances demand bathing, it is important to keep them in a warm spot while they are wet. Young animals are more susceptible to drafts than older ones. 2) Scissoring is normally the only type of clipping your Dobe will require. 3) Your veterinarian can show you the most efficient method of "pilling" your dog.

2

3

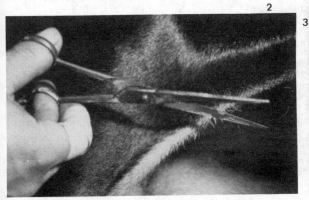

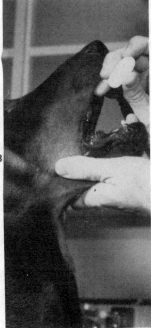

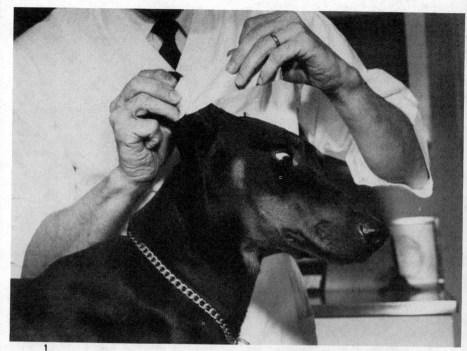

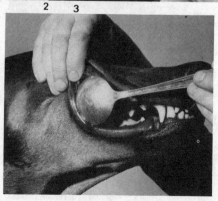

1) Ear cropping, as well as tail docking, is usually a job for the veterinarian. Here a vet puts new bandages on this young Dobe's ears in the final stages of training the ears upright. There are alternative methods of giving a dog liquid medicine; 2) shows a cup being used, while in 3) medicine is administered from a spoon. In either case, administering from the side of the mouth is generally more efficient than approaching from the front.

If you have chosen your Dobe puppy with an eye toward showing him, fundamentals of show training should begin early.

send you a new certificate. If you receive, instead, an application for registration, you should fill it out choosing a name for your dog, and mail it, with the fee, to the A.K.C.

The pedigree is a chart showing your puppy's ancestry and is not a part of his official papers. The health certificate will tell what shots have been given and when the next ones are due. Your veterinarian will be appreciative of this information, and will continue with the same series of shots, if they have not been completed. The health certificate will also give the date on which the puppy has been wormed.

REGISTERING YOUR DOBE PUPPY

For information on how to register a new litter of pedigreed dogs owners may write to the following:

American Kennel Club
51 Madison Ave.
New York, N.Y. 10010

Canadian Kennel Club
111 Eglinton Avenue East
Toronto 12, Ontario
Canada

Australian Kennel Club
Royal Show Grounds
Ascot Vale, Victoria
Australia

British Kennel Club
1 Clarges Street
Picadilly, London W.1
England

THE DOBE PUPPY'S FIRST NIGHT WITH YOU

The puppy's first night at home is likely to be disturbing to the family. Keep in mind that suddenly being away from his mother, brothers and sisters is a new experience for him; he may be confused and frightened. If you have a special room in which you have his bed, be sure that there is nothing there with which he can harm himself. Be sure that all lamp cords are out of his reach and that there is nothing that he can tip or pull over. Check furniture that he might get stuck under or behind and objects that he might chew. If you want him to sleep in your room he probably will be quiet all night, reassured by your presence. If left in a room by himself he will cry and howl, and you will have to steel yourself to be impervious to his whining. After a few nights alone he should adjust. The first night that he is alone it is wise to put a loud-ticking alarm clock, as well as his toys, in the room with him. The alarm clock will make a comforting noise, and he will not feel that he is alone.

YOUR DOBERMAN PUPPY'S BED

Every dog likes to have a place that is his alone. He holds nothing more sacred than his own bed whether it be a rug, dog crate, or dog bed. If you get your puppy a bed be sure to get one which discourages chewing. Also be sure that the bed is large enough to be comfortable for him when he is full grown. Locate it away from drafts and radiators. A word might be said here in defense of the crate, which many pet owners think is cruel and confining. Given a choice, a young dog instinctively selects a secure place in which to lounge, rest or sleep. The walls and ceiling of a crate, even a wire one, answer that need. Once he regards his crate as a safe and reassuring place to stay, you will be able to leave him alone in the house.

FEEDING YOUR DOBERMAN PUPPY

At the time of purchase, most breeders will give you food for a few days, along with instructions for feeding so that your puppy will have the same diet he is accustomed to until you can buy a supply at your pet shop.

As a general rule, a puppy from weaning time (six weeks) to three months of age should be fed four meals a day; from three months to six months, three meals; from six months to one year, two meals. After a year, a dog does well on one meal daily. There are as many feeding schedules as there are breeders, and puppies do fine on all of them, so it is best for the new owner to follow the one given him by the breeder of his puppy. Remember that all dogs are individuals. The amount that will keep your dog in good health is right for him, not the "rule book" amount. A feeding schedule to give you some idea of what the average puppy will eat is as follows:

Morning meal: Puppy meal with milk.

Afternoon meal: Meat mixed with puppy meal, plus a vitamin-mineral supplement.

Evening meal: Same as afternoon meal, but without a vitamin-mineral supplement.

Do not change the amounts in your puppy's diet too rapidly. If he gets diarrhea it may be that he is eating too much, so cut back on his food and when he is normal again increase his food more slowly.

There is a canned food made especially for puppies which you can buy with a veterinarian's prescription, and several commercially prepared products. Some breeders use this method very successfully from weaning to three months.

Puppies are usually completely weaned from the mother dog by the time they are six weeks old. They should have been introduced to soft solids by this time and within a couple more weeks should be eating four meals a day with no supplementary nursings from the dam.

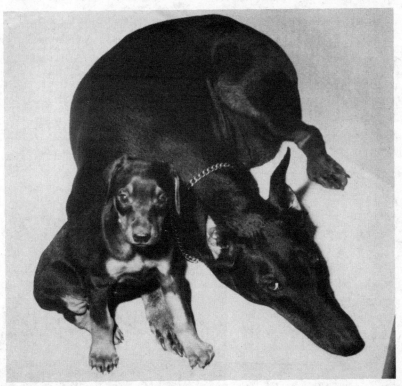

1

2

3

1) A Doberman pup in the preliminary phase of obedience training balks at complying with the "come" command. 2) Trainer has leather arm guard laced into place prior to beginning attack training. 3) Young adult dog shows he knows what is expected of him during a session of guard training. 4) Training for the "come" command consists of putting your dog on a generous length of leash and standing a distance from him while giving the command and gently pulling on the lead to make him comply. 5) Two members of an accomplished Doberman drill team sport their monogrammed jackets while waiting for the next exercise. 6) Pup during training for "come" command is being pulled to his feet, and finally 7) urged, via pressure applied to leash, to come to the trainer.

TRANSITIONAL DIET

Changing over to an adult program of feeding is not difficult. Very often the puppy will change himself: that is, he will refuse to eat some of his meals. He'll adjust to his one meal (or two meals) a day without any trouble at all.

BREAKING TO COLLAR AND LEASH

Puppies are usually broken to a collar before you bring them home, but even if yours has never worn one it is a simple matter to get him used to it. Put a loose collar on him for a few hours. At first he may scratch at it and try to get it off, but gradually he will take it as a matter of course. To break him to a lead, attach his leash to his collar and let him drag it around. When he becomes used to it pick it up and gently pull him in the direction you want him to go. He will think it is a game, and with a bit of patience on your part he will allow himself to be led.

DISCIPLINING YOUR DOBERMAN PUPPY

The way to have a well-mannered adult dog is to give him firm basic training while he is a puppy. When you say "No" you must mean "No." Your dog will respect you only if you are firm. A six-to eight-week-old puppy is old enough to understand what "No" means. The first time you see your puppy doing something he shouldn't be doing, chewing something he shouldn't chew or wandering in a forbidden area, it's time to teach him. Say "No" firmly. Usually a firm "No" in a disapproving tone of voice is enough to correct your dog, but occasionally you get a puppy that requires a firmer hand, especially as he grows older. In this case hold your puppy firmly and slap him gently across the hindquarters. If this seems cruel, you should realize that no dog resents being disciplined if he is caught in the act of doing something wrong, and your puppy will be intelligent enough to know what the slap was for.

After you have slapped him and you can see that he has learned his lesson, call him to you and talk to him in a pleasant tone of voice—praise him for coming to you. This sounds contradictory, but it works with a puppy. He immediately forgives you, practically tells you that it was his fault and that he deserved his punishment, and promises that it will not happen again. This form of discipline works best and may be used for all misbehaviors.

Never punish your puppy by chasing him around, making occasional swipes with a rolled-up newspaper: punish him only when you have a firm hold on him. Above all, never punish you dog after having called him to you. He must learn to associate coming to you with something pleasant.

HOUSEBREAKING

While housebreaking your puppy, do not let him have the run of the house. If you do you will find that he will pick out his own bathroom, which may be in your bedroom or in the middle of the living room rug. Keep him confined to a small area where you can watch him, and you will be able to train him much more easily and speedily. A puppy does not want to dirty his bed, but he does need to be taught where he should go. Spread papers over his living quarters, then watch him carefully. When you notice him starting to whimper, sniff the floor or run agitatedly in little circles, rush him to the place that you want to serve as his relief area and gently hold him there until he relieves himself. Then praise him lavishly. When you remove the soiled papers, leave a small damp piece so that the puppy's sense of smell will lead him back there next time. If he makes a mistake, wash the area at once with warm water, followed by a rinse with water and vinegar or sudsy ammonia. This will kill the odor and prevent discoloration. It shouldn't take more than a few days for him to get the idea of using newspapers. When he becomes fairly consistent, reduce the area of paper to a few sheets in a corner. As soon as you think he has the idea fixed in his mind, you can let him roam around the house a bit, but keep an eye on him. It might be best to keep him on a leash the first few days so that you can rush him back to his paper at any signs of an approaching accident.

The normal healthy puppy will want to relieve himself when he wakes up in the morning, after each feeding and after strenuous exercise. During early puppyhood any excitement, such as the return home of a member of the family or the approach of a visitor, may result in floor-wetting, but that phase should pass in a few weeks. Keep in mind that you can't expect too much from your puppy until he is about five months old. Before that, his muscles and digestive system just aren't under his control.

OUTDOOR HOUSEBREAKING

You can begin outdoor training on a leash even while you are paper-training your puppy. First thing in the morning take him outdoors (to the curb, if you are in the city) and walk him back and forth in a small area until he relieves himself. He will probably make a puddle and then walk around, uncertain of what is expected of him. You can try standing him over a newspaper, which may give him the idea. Praise your dog every time taking him outside brings results, and he will get the idea. You'll find, when you begin the outdoor training, that the male puppy usually requires a longer walk than the female. Both male and female puppies will squat. It isn't until he is older that the male dog will begin to lift his leg. If you hate to give up your sleep, you can train your puppy to go outdoors during the day and use the paper at night.

ALL DOGS NEED TO CHEW

Puppies and young dogs need something with resistance to chew on while their teeth and jaws are developing—for cutting the puppy teeth, to induce growth of the permanent teeth under the puppy teeth, to assist in getting rid of the puppy teeth at the proper time, to help the permanent teeth through the gums, to assure normal jaw development and to settle the permanent teeth solidly in the jaws.

The adult dog's desire to chew stems from the instinct for tooth cleaning, gum massage and jaw exercise—plus the need for an outlet for periodic doggie tensions.

Dental caries as it affects the teeth of humans is virtually unknown in dogs—but tartar accumulates on the teeth of dogs, particularly at the gum line, more rapidly than on the teeth of humans. These accumulations, if not removed, bring irritation, and then infection which erodes the tooth enamel and ultimately destroys the teeth at the roots. Most chewing by adult dogs is an effort to do something about this problem for themselves.

Tooth and jaw development will normally continue until the dog is more than a year old—but sometimes much longer, depending upon the breed, chewing exercise, the rate at which calcium can be utilized and many other factors, known and unknown, which affect the development of individual dogs. Diseases, like distemper for example, may sometimes arrest development of the teeth and jaws, which may resume months, or even years later.

This is why dogs, especially puppies and young dogs, will often destroy property worth hundreds of dollars, when their chewing instinct is not diverted from their owner's possessions, particularly during the widely varying critical period for young dogs.

Saving your possessions from destruction, assuring proper development of teeth and jaws, providing for 'interim' tooth cleaning and gum massage, and channeling doggie tensions into a non-destructive outlet are, therefore, all dependent upon the dog having something suitable for chewing readily available when his instinct tells him to chew. If your purposes, and those of your dog, are to be accomplished, what you provide for chewing must be desirable from the doggie viewpoint, have the necessary functional qualities, and above all, be safe for your dog.

It is very important that dogs not be permitted to chew on anything they can break, or indigestible things from which they can bite sizeable chunks. Sharp pieces, from such as a bone which can be broken by a dog, may pierce the intestine wall and kill. Indigestible things which can be

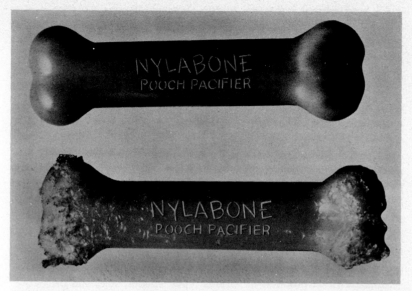

Nylabone®, a unique 100 percent nylon chew bone, is the perfect chewing pacifier for young dogs in their teething stage, or even for older dogs to help satisfy that occasional urge to chew. Unlike many other dog bones on the market today, Nylabone® does not splinter or fall apart. It will last indefinitely and as it is used it frills, becoming a doggie toothbrush that cleans teeth and massages gums.

bitten off in chunks, such as toys made of rubber compound or cheap plastic, may cause an intestinal stoppage, if not regurgitated—to bring painful death, unless surgery is promptly performed.

Strong natural bones, such as 4 to 8 inch lengths of round shin bone from mature beef—either the kind you can get from your butcher or one of the variety available commercially in pet stores—may serve your dog's teething needs, if his mouth is large enough to handle them effectively.

You may be tempted to give your puppy a smaller bone and he may not be able to break it when you do—but puppies grow rapidly and the power of their jaws constantly increases until maturity. This means that a growing dog may break one of the smaller bones at any time, swallow the pieces and die painfully before you realize what is wrong.

Many people make the mistake of thinking of their dog's teeth in terms of the teeth of the wild carnivores or those of the dog in antiquity. The teeth of the wild carnivorous animals, and the teeth found in the fossils of the dog-like creatures of antiquity, have far thicker and stronger enamel than those of our contemporary dogs.

All hard natural bones are highly abrasive. If your dog is an avid chewer, natural bones may wear away his teeth prematurely; hence, they then should be taken away from your dog when the teething purposes have been served. The badly worn, and usually painful, teeth of many mature dogs can be traced to excessive chewing on natural bones.

Contrary to popular belief, knuckle bones which can be chewed up and swallowed by the dog provide little, if any, useable calcium or other nutriment. They do, however, disturb the digestion of most dogs and cause them to vomit the nourishing food they need.

An old leather shoe is another popular answer to the chewing need—but be very sure that the rubber heel, all nails, and other metal parts such as lace grommets, metal arches, etc., have been removed. Be especially careful to get all of the nails. A chunk of rubber heel can cause an intestinal stoppage. If it has a nail in it, the intestine wall may be pierced or torn. Then there is, of course, always the hazard that your dog may fail to differentiate between his shoe and yours, and eat up a good pair while you're not looking.

Dried rawhide products of various types, shapes, sizes and prices are available on the market and have become quite popular. However, they don't serve the primary chewing functions very well; they are a bit messy when wet from mouthing, and most dogs chew them up rather rapidly—but they have been considered safe for dogs until recently. Now, more and more incidents of death, and near death, by strangulation have been reported to be the result of partially swallowed chunks of rawhide swelling in the throat. More recently, some veterinarians have been attributing cases of acute constipation to large pieces of incompletely digested rawhide in the intestine.

The nylon bones, especially those with natural meat and bone fractions added, are probably the most complete, safe and economical answer to the chewing need. Dogs cannot break them or bite off sizeable chunks; hence, they are completely safe—and being longer lasting than other things offered for the purpose, they are economical.

Hard chewing raises little bristle-like projections on the surface of the nylon bones—to provide effective interim tooth cleaning and vigorous gum massage, much in the same way your tooth brush does it for you. The little projections are raked off and swallowed in the form of thin shavings—but the chemistry of the nylon is such that they break down in the stomach fluids and pass through without effect.

The toughness of the nylon provides the strong chewing resistance needed for important jaw exercise and effective help for the teething functions—but there is no tooth wear because nylon is non-abrasive. Being inert, nylon does not support the growth of microorganisms—and it can be washed in soap and water, or it can be sterilized by boiling or in an autoclave.

Nylabone® is highly recommended by veterinarians as a safe, healthy nylon bone that can't splinter or chip. Instead, Nylabone is frizzled by the dog's chewing action, creating a toothbrush-like surface that cleanses the teeth and massages the gums. Nylabone® and Nylaball®, the only chew products made of flavor-impregnated solid nylon, are available in your local pet shop.

Nothing, however, substitutes for periodic professional attention to your dog's teeth and gums, not any more than your toothbrush can do that for you. Have your dog's teeth cleaned by your veterinarian at least once a year, twice a year is better—and he will be healthier, happier and far more pleasant to live with.

Nylaball®, another fully nylon dog pacifier, is a hygienic chew product that will hold your dog's interest for hours. Impregnated with ham flavor, it is a wholly safe, long-lasting product that cannot endanger your dog's life with the threat of fragments that may become lodged in his throat.

5. OBEDIENCE TRAINING

WHEN TO START TRAINING

You should never begin *serious* obedience training before your dog is seven or eight months old. (Some animal psychologists state that puppies can begin training when seven weeks old, if certain techniques are followed. These techniques, however, are still experimental and should be left to the professional trainer.) While your dog is still in his early puppyhood, concentrate on winning his confidence so he will love and admire you. Basic training can be started at the age of three or four months. He should be taught to walk nicely on a leash, sit and lie down on command, and come when he is called.

YOUR PART IN TRAINING

You must patiently demonstrate to your dog what each word of command means. Guide him with your hands and the training leash, reassuring him with your voice, through whatever routine you are teaching him. Repeat the word associated with the act. Demonstrate again and again to give the dog a chance to make the connection in his mind.

Once he begins to get the idea, use the word of command without any physical guidance. Drill him. When he makes mistakes, correct him, kindly at first, more severely as his training progresses. Try not to lose your patience or become irritated, and never slap him with your hand or the leash during the training session. Withholding praise or rebuking him will make him feel bad enough.

When he does what you want, praise him lavishly with words and with pats. Don't continually reward with dog candy or treats in training. The dog that gets into the habit of performing for a treat will seldom be fully dependable when he can't smell or see one in the offing. When he carries out a command, even though his performance is slow or sloppy, praise him and he will perform more readily the next time.

THE TRAINING VOICE

When you start training your dog, use your training voice, giving commands in a firm, clear tone. Once you give a command, persist until it is obeyed, even if you have to pull the dog to obey you. He must learn that training is different from playing, that a command once given must be obeyed no matter what distractions are present. Remember that the tone and pitch of your voice, not loudness, are the qualities that will influence your dog most.

Be consistent in the use of words during training. Confine your commands to as few words as possible and never change them. It is best for only one person to carry on the dog's training, because different people will use different words and tactics that will confuse your dog. The dog who hears "come," "get over here," "hurry up," "here, Rex," and other commands when he is wanted will become totally confused.

TRAINING LESSONS

Training is hard on the dog and the trainer. A young dog just cannot take more than ten minutes of training at a stretch, so limit the length of your first lessons. Then you can gradually increase the length of time to about thirty minutes. You'll find that you too will tend to become impatient when you stretch out a training lesson. If you find yourself losing your temper, stop and resume the lesson at another time. Before and after each lesson have a play period, but don't play during a training session. Even the youngest dog soon learns that schooling is a serious matter; fun comes afterward.

Don't spend too much time on one phase of training, or the dog will become bored. Always try to end a lesson on a pleasant note. Actually, in nine cases out of ten, if your dog isn't doing what you want it's because you're not getting the idea over to him properly.

YOUR TRAINING EQUIPMENT AND ITS USE

The leash is more properly called the lead, so we'll use that term here. The best leads for training are the six-foot webbed-cloth leads, usually olive-drab in color, and the six-foot leather lead. Fancier leads are available and may be used if desired.

You'll need a metal-link collar, called a choke chain, consisting of a metal chain with rings on each end. Even though the name may sound frightening, it won't hurt your dog, and it is an absolute MUST in training. There is a right and a wrong way to put the training collar on. It should go around the dog's neck so that you can attach the lead to the ring at the end of the chain which passes over, not under the neck. It is most important that the collar is put on properly so it will tighten when the lead is pulled and ease when you relax your grip.

The correct way to hold the lead is also very important, as the collar should have some slack in it at all times, except when correcting. Holding the loop in your right hand, extend your arm out to the side, even with your shoulder. With your left hand, grasp the lead as close as possible to the collar, without making it tight. The remaining portion of the lead can

Your local pet store is the source of a large selection of leads and collars that can be used for training or showing, or just taking your pet for a walk. Since puppies quickly outgrow their first collars and leads, plan to purchase at least two sets of equipment.

be made into a loop which is held in the right hand. Keep this arm close to your body. Most corrections will be made with the left hand by giving the lead a jerk in the direction you want the dog to go.

HEELING

"Heeling" in dog language means having your dog walk alongside you on your left side, close to your leg, on lead or off. With patience and effort you can train your dog to walk with you even on a crowded street or in the presence of other dogs.

Now that you have learned the correct way to put on your dog's collar and how to hold the lead, you are ready to start with his first lesson in heeling. Make the dog sit at your left side. Using the dog's name and the command "Heel," start forward on your LEFT foot, giving a tug on the lead to get the dog started. Always use the dog's name first, followed by the command, such as "Rex, heel." Saying his name will help get his attention and will let him know that you are about to give a command.

Walk briskly, with even steps, going around in a large circle, square or straight line. While walking, make sure that your dog stays on the left side and close to your leg. If he lags behind, snap gently on the lead to get him up to you, then praise him lavishly for doing well. If he forges ahead or swings wide, stop and jerk the lead sharply and bring him back to the proper position. Always praise him when he returns to the correct place. As soon as you have snapped the lead to correct your dog, let it go slack again at the desired length. Don't drag the dog or keep the lead taut as this will develop into a tug of war which is ineffective.

To keep your dog's attention, talk to him as you keep him in place. You can also do a series of fast about-turns, giving the lead a jerk as you turn. He will gradually learn that he must pay attention or be jerked to your side. You can vary the routine by changing speeds, doing turns, figure-eights, and by zig-zagging across the training area.

"HEEL" MEANS "SIT," TOO

To the dog, the command "Heel" will also mean that he has to sit in the heel position at your left side when you stop walking with no additional command from you. As you practice heeling, make him sit whenever you stop, at first using the word "Sit," then with no command at all. He'll soon get the idea and sit down when you stop and wait for the command "Heel" to start walking again.

TRAINING TO SIT

Training your dog to sit should be fairly easy. Stand him on your left side, holding the lead fairly short, and command him to "Sit." As you give the verbal command, pull up slightly with the lead and push his hindquarters down. Do not let him lie down or stand up. If he does lie down, snap up on the lead until he rises to a sitting position again. If he is slow to respond, tug more sharply until he has done what you want him to. Keep him in a sitting position for a moment, then release the pressure on the lead and praise him. Constantly repeat the command as you hold him in a sitting position, thus fitting the word to the action in his mind. If he moves at all, immediately repeat the command and press him into a sitting position. After a time he will begin to get the idea and will sit without having to push his hindquarters down. When he reaches that stage, insist that he sit on command. Praise him often, always rewarding a correct action with your praise and affection.

THE "LIE DOWN" OR "DOWN"

The object of this is to get the dog to lie down either on the verbal command "Down" or when you give the hand signal, your hand raised in front of you, palm down. However, until the dog is really sure of the meaning of the command, and will do it by himself with no forcible action from you, the hand signal should only be used to accompany the verbal command. This command may be more difficult at first because it places the dog in a defenseless position, which may cause him to bolt away. Be lavish with your praise and affection when he has assumed the correct position and he will soon learn that nothing bad happens to him, and on the contrary will associate the "Down" position with pleasing his master or mistress.

Don't start training to lie down until the dog is almost letter-perfect in sitting on command. Place the dog in a sit, and kneel before him. With both hands, reach forward to his legs and take one front leg in each hand, thumbs up, holding just above the elbows. Lift his legs slightly off the ground and pull them somewhat out in front of him. Simultaneously, give the command "Down" and lower his front legs to the ground.

Hold the dog down and stroke him to let him know that staying down is what you want him to do. This method is far better than forcing a young dog down. Using force can cause him to become very frightened and he will begin to dislike any training. Always talk to your dog and let him know that you are very pleased with him, and soon you will find that you have a happy working dog.

After he begins to get the idea, slide the lead under your left foot and give the command "Down." At the same time, pull the lead. This will help get the dog down. Meanwhile, raise your hand in the down signal. Don't expect to accomplish all this in one session. Be patient and work with the dog. He'll cooperate if you show him just what you expect him to do.

THE "STAY"

The next step is to train your dog to stay either in a "Sit" or "Down" position. As before, use the lead to teach this command until your dog is responding perfectly to your instruction, then you may try it off the lead. To begin with the Sit-Stay, place your dog in a sitting position beside you in the automatic heel-sit position. Holding the leash in one hand (most trainers prefer the left), take a long step forward and turn to face him holding your free hand open, palm toward him, fingers pointing downward, in front of his nose and speak the command "Stay." If he offers to follow you, as it would be natural for him to do since this has been his ready position for heel, snap up on the lead to return him to the sit, put your hand in front of his face and repeat the command firmly once more. Allow him to remain sitting for a few seconds before going through the procedure again. Each time he successfully performs, praise him profusely and show him you are pleased with him.

Repeat this procedure until your dog behaves as if he understands what is expected of him. When he has mastered this procedure, step away to the right of him, then behind, then a few steps forward, a few steps to the side, and so on, until you have gone the full length of the leash. Anytime your dog offers to follow you, snap upward on the leash, extending your arm palm forward to him and repeat the command sharply. When he has demonstrated a willingness to remain in the correct position while you walk the full extent of the lead, you are ready to train him to remain in position using a longer length of cord, about 25 or 30 feet, and finally the Sit-Stay off the lead.

Once the Sit-Stay is learned, you can teach the Down-Stay by beginning with the Down command, then apply approximately the same methods as in the Sit-Stay.

THE COME ON COMMAND

You can train your dog to come when you call him if you begin when he is young. At first, work with him on lead. Sit the dog, then back away the length of the lead and call him, putting into your voice as much coaxing affection as possible. Give an easy tug on the lead to get him started. When he does come, make a big fuss over him—it might help at this point to give him a small piece of dog candy or food as a reward. He should get the idea soon. You can also move away from him the full length of the lead and call to him something like "Rex, come," then run backward a few steps and stop, making him sit directly in front of you.

Don't be too eager to practice coming on command off lead. Wait until you are certain that you have the dog under perfect control before you try calling him when he's free. Once he gets the idea that he can disobey a command and get away with it, your training program will suffer a serious setback. Keep in mind that your dog's life may depend on his immediate response to a command to come when he is called. If he disobeys off lead, put the lead back on and correct him severely with jerks of the lead.

TEACHING TO COME TO HEEL

The object of this is for you to stand still, say "Heel," and have your dog come right over to you and sit by your left knee in the heel position. If your dog has been trained to sit without command every time you stop, he's ready for this step.

Sit him in front of and facing you and step back one step. Moving only your left foot, pull the dog behind you, then step forward and pull him around until he is in a heel position. You can also have the dog go around by passing the lead behind your back. Use your left heel to straighten him out if he begins to sit behind you or crookedly. This may take a little work, but he will get the idea if you show him just what you want.

THE STAND

Your dog should be trained to stand in one spot without moving his feet, and he should allow a stranger to run his hand over his body and legs without showing any resentment or fear. Employ the same method you used in training him to stay on the sit and down. While walking, place your left hand out, palm toward his nose, and command him to stay. His first impulse will be to sit, so be prepared to stop him by placing your hand under his body, near his hindquarters, and holding him until he gets the idea that this is different from the command to sit. Praise him for standing, then walk to the end of the lead. Correct him strongly if he starts to move. Have a stranger approach him and run his hands over the dog's back and down his legs. Keep him standing until you come back to him. Walk around him from his left side, come to the heel position, and make sure that he does not sit until you command him to. This is a very valuable exercise. If you plan to show your dog, he will have to learn to stand in a show pose and allow the judge to examine him. The judge will run his hands along the dog's back and down the legs, so it is important that the dog stands calmly and steadfastly.

TRAINING SCHOOLS AND CLASSES

There are dog training schools in all parts of the country, some sponsored by the local humane society.

If you feel that you lack the time or the skill to train your dog yourself, there are professional dog trainers who will do it for you, but basically dog training is a matter of training YOU and your dog to work together as a team, and if you don't do it yourself you will miss a lot of fun. Don't give up after trying unsuccessfully for a short time. Try a little harder and you and your dog will be able to work things out.

ADVANCED TRAINING AND OBEDIENCE TRIALS

Once you begin training your dog and you see how well he does, you'll probably be bitten by the "obedience bug"—the desire to enter him in obedience trials held under American Kennel Club auspices.

The A.K.C. obedience trials are divided into three classes: Novice, Open and Utility.

In trials for advanced obedience degrees, your dog will have to successfully accomplish two scent discrimination exercises. From among several objects like the ones above, he will have to choose the one that has been touched by his handler or owner and carries that person's scent.

In the Novice Class the dog will be judged on the following basis:

TEST MAXIMUM SCORE

Heel on lead 40
Stand for examination 30
Heel free—off lead 40
Recall (come on command) 30
One-minute sit (handler in ring) 30
Three-minute down (handler in ring) 30
Maximum total score 200

If the dog "qualifies" in three shows by earning at least 50% of the points for each test, with a total of at least 170 for the trial, he has earned the Companion Dog degree and the letters C.D. (Companion Dog) are entered after his name in the American Kennel Club records.

The hurdle is used in different events in advanced obedience competition. It figures in the single jump, in the retrieve, and in the directed jump. The bar is adjustable, so that the height a dog must jump to successfully accomplish the particular exercise will be proportional to his size. Informal hurdles can be simulated out of a variety of different items for backyard or indoor practice before the actual trial.

After the dog has earned his Companion Dog title, he is eligible to enter the Open Class competition and compete for his next degree. He will be judged on this basis:

TEST MAXIMUM SCORE

Heel free 40

Drop on recall 30

Retrieve (wooden dumbbell) on flat 20

Retrieve over obstacle (hurdle) 30

Broad jump 20

Three-minute sit (handler out of ring) 30

Five-minute down (handler out of ring) 30

Maximum total score 200

Again he must qualify in three shows for the C.D.X. (Companion Dog Excellent) title, earning at least 50% of the points for each test, with a total of at least 170 for the trial. He is then eligible to compete in the Utility Class, where he can earn the Utility Dog (U.D.) degree in these rugged tests:

TEST MAXIMUM SCORE

Scent discrimination (picking up article handled by master from group) Article 1 30

Scent discrimination Article 2 30

Directed Retrieve 30

Signal exercise (heeling, etc., on hand signal) 40

Directed jumping (over hurdle and bar jump) 40

Group examination 30

Maximum total score 200

For more complete information about these obedience trials, write for the American Kennel Club's *Regulations and Standards for Obedience Trials.* Dogs that are disqualified from breed shows because of neutering or physical defects are eligible to compete in these trials. Besides the formal A.K.C. obedience trials, there are informal "match" trials in which dogs compete for ribbons and inexpensive trophies. These shows are run by many local fanciers' clubs and by all-breed obedience clubs. In many localities the humane society and other groups conduct their own obedience shows. Your local newspaper, pet shop proprietor or kennel club can keep you informed about such shows in your vicinity, and you will find them listed in the different dog magazines or in the pet column of your paper.

6. BREEDING YOUR DOG

THE QUESTION OF SPAYING

If you feel that you will never want to raise a litter of purebred puppies, and if you do not wish to risk the possibility of an undesirable mating and surplus mongrel puppies inevitably destined for euthanasia at the local pound, you may want to have your female spayed. Spaying is generally best performed after the female has passed her first heat and before her first birthday; this allows the female to attain the normal female characteristics, while still being young enough to avoid the possible complications encountered when an older female is spayed. A spayed female will remain a healthy, lively pet. You often hear that an altered female will become very fat. However, if you cut down on her food intake, she will not gain weight.

On the other hand, if you wish to show your dog in American Kennel Club competition (altered females are disqualified) or enjoy the excitement and feeling of accomplishment of breeding and raising a litter of quality puppies, particularly in your breed and from your pet, then do not spay your dog until a more appropriate time.

Male dogs are almost never altered (castrated) unless they exhibit excessive sexual tendencies.

SEXUAL PHYSIOLOGY

Females usually reach sexual maturity (indicated by the first heat cycle, or season) at eight or nine months of age, but sexual maturity may occur as early as six months or as late as thirteen months of age. Generally, the larger the breed is the longer it takes to reach full maturity.

The average heat cycle (estrus period) lasts for twenty or twenty-one days, and occurs approximately every six months. For about five days immediately preceeding the heat period, the female generally displays restlessness and an increased appetite. The vulva, or external genitals, begins to swell. The discharge, which is bright red at the onset and gradually becomes pale pink to straw in color, increases in quantity for several days and then slowly subsides, finally ceasing altogether. The vaginal discharge is subject to much variation; in some bitches it is quite heavy, in others it may never appear, and in some it may be so slight as to go unnoticed.

About eight or nine days after the first appearance of the discharge, the female becomes very playful with other dogs, but will not allow a mating

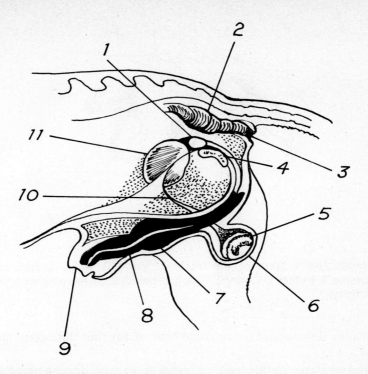

Reproductive system of a male dog: 1. Prostate 2. Rectum 3. Anus
4. Section of pelvic bone 5. Testicle 6. Scrotum 7. Bulb (part of Penis)
8. Penis 9. Sheath 10. Vas deferens 11. Bladder.

to take place. Anywhere from the tenth or eleventh day to the seventeenth
or eighteenth day, the female will accept males and be able to conceive.
Many biologists apply the term "heat" only to this receptive phase rather
than to the whole estrus period, as is commonly done by dog fanciers.

The ova (egg cells) from the female's ovaries are discharged into the
oviduct toward the close of the acceptance phase, usually the sixteenth to
eighteenth day. From the eighteenth day until the end of the cycle, the
female is still attractive to males, but she will repulse their advances. The
entire estrus, however, may be quite variable; in some females vaginal
bleeding ends and mating begins on the fourth day; in others the
discharge may continue throughout the entire cycle and the female will
not accept males until the seventeenth day or even later.

The male dog—simply referred to by fanciers as the "dog" or "stud,"
in contrast to the female, which is referred to as the "bitch"—upon
reaching sexual maturity, usually at about six to eight months, is able,

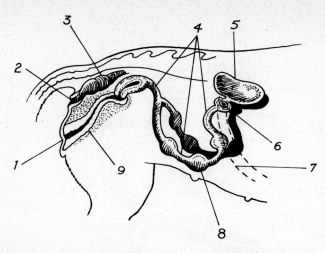

Reproductive system of the bitch: 1. Vulva 2. Anus 3. Rectum 4. Uterus 5. Kidney 6. Ovary 7. Ribs (indicated) 8. Developing embryo 9. Vagina.

like other domesticated mammals, to breed at any time throughout the year.

The testes, the sperm-producing organs of the male, descend from the body cavity into the scrotum at birth. The condition of cryptorchidism refers to the retention of one or both testes within the body cavity. A testicle retained within the body cavity is in an environment too hot for it to function normally. A retained testicle may also become cancerous. If only one testicle descends, the dog is known as a monorchid; if neither descends, the dog is known as an anorchid (dog fanciers, however, refer to a dog with the latter condition as a cryptorchid). A monorchid dog is a fertile animal; an anorchid is sterile.

The male dog's penis has a bulbous enlargement at its base and, in addition, like the penis of a number of other mammals, contains a bone. When mating occurs, pressure on the penis causes a reflex action that fills the bulb with blood, swelling it to five times its normal size within the female. This locks, or ties, the two animals together. After ejaculation, the animals usually remain tied for fifteen to thirty minutes. However, they may separate very quickly or remain together an hour or more, depending on the length of time for the blood to drain from the bulb.

CARE OF THE FEMALE IN ESTRUS

If you have a dog-proof run within your yard, it will be safe to leave your female in season there; if you don't have such a run, she should be shut indoors. Don't leave her alone outside even for a minute; she should be exercised only on lead. If you want to prevent the neighborhood dogs from congregating around your doorstep, as they inevitably will as soon as they discover that your female is in season, take her some distance from the house before you let her relieve herself. Take her in your car to a park or field for a chance to "stretch" her legs (always on lead, of course). Keep watch for male dogs, and if one approaches take the female back to the car. After the three weeks are up you can let her out as before with no worry that she can have puppies until her next season.

Some owners find it simpler to board their female at a kennel until her season is over. However, it really is not difficult to watch your female at home. There are various products on the market which are useful at this time. Although the female in season keeps herself quite clean, sometimes she unavoidably stains furniture or rugs. You can buy sanitary belts made expecially for dogs at your pet shop. Consult your veterinarian for information on pills to be taken to check odor during this period. There also is a pill that prevents the female from coming in season for extended periods, and there are many different types of liquids, powders and sprays of varying efficiency used to keep male dogs away. However, the

There are several products on the market designed to make life easier for both you and your bitch during the estrus cycle. Sanitary pads for dogs are one of these items and come complete with a belt for holding the pad in place.

one safe rule (whatever products you use) is: keep your bitch away from dogs that could mount her.

SHOULD YOU BREED YOUR MALE?

Deciding whether or not to use a male dog as a stud is a question with two sides. The arguments for and against using a dog as a stud are often very close to ridiculous. A classic example would be the tale that once you use a dog as a stud he will lose his value as a show dog or any one of the other functions a dog may have. A sound rule may well be: if you have a stud who has proven his worth at the shows, place his services out for hire, if only for the betterment of the breed; if your dog is not of show quality, do not use him as a stud.

Top champion studs can bring their owners many dollars in breeding revenue. If the stud is as good as you feel he is, his services will soon be in great demand. Using a dog as a stud will not lower his value in other functions in any way. Many breeders will permit a male dog to breed an experienced female once, when about a year old, and then they begin to show their stud until he has gained his conformation championship. He is then placed out for hire through advertising in the various bulletins, journals and show catalogues, and through the stud registers maintained by many pet shops and kennel clubs.

SHOULD YOU BREED YOUR FEMALE?

If you are an amateur and decide to breed your female it would be wise to talk with a breeder and find out all that breeding and caring for puppies entails. You must be prepared to assume the responsibility of caring for the mother through her pregnancy and for the puppies until they are of saleable age. Raising a litter of puppies can be a rewarding experience, but it means work as well as fun, and there is no guarantee of financial profit. As the puppies grow older and require more room and care, the amateur breeder, in desperation, often sells the puppies for much less than they are worth; sometimes he has to give them away. If the cost of keeping the puppies will drain your finances, think twice.

If you have given careful consideration to all these things and still want to breed your female, remember that there is some preparation necessary before taking this step.

WHEN TO BREED

It is usually best to breed in the second or third season of your bitch. Consider when the puppies will be born and whether their birth and later care will interfere with your work or vacation plans. Gestation period is approximately fifty-eight to sixty-five days. Allow enough time to select

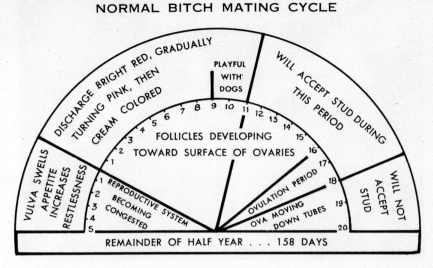

NORMAL BITCH MATING CYCLE

DISCHARGE BRIGHT RED, GRADUALLY
TURNING PINK, THEN
CREAM COLORED

PLAYFUL WITH DOGS

WILL ACCEPT STUD DURING
THIS PERIOD

FOLLICLES DEVELOPING
TOWARD SURFACE OF OVARIES

3 4 5 6 7 8 9 10 11 12 13 14 15 16 17 18 19 20
1 2

VULVA SWELLS
APPETITE INCREASES
RESTLESSNESS

REPRODUCTIVE SYSTEM
BECOMING
CONGESTED

OVULATION PERIOD
OVA MOVING
DOWN TUBES

WILL NOT ACCEPT STUD

REMAINDER OF HALF YEAR . . . 158 DAYS

the right stud for her. Don't be in a position of having to settle for any available stud if she comes into season sooner than expected. Your female will probably be ready to breed twelve days after the first colored discharge. You can usually make arrangements to board her with the owner of the male for a few days to insure her being there at the proper time, or you can take her to be mated and bring her home the same day. If she still appears receptive she may be bred again a day or two later. Some females never show signs of willingness, so it helps to have the experience of a breeder. The second day after the discharge changes color is the proper time; she may be bred for about three days following. For an additional week or so she may have some discharge and attract other dogs by her odor, but she can seldom be bred at this time.

HOW TO SELECT A STUD

Choose a mate for your female with an eye to countering her deficiencies. If possible, both male and female should have several ancestors in common within the last two or three generations, as such combinations generally "click" best. The male should have a good show record himself or be the sire of champions. The owner of the stud usually charges a fee for the use of the dog. The fee varies. Payment of a fee does not guarantee a litter, but it does generally confer the right to breed your female again to the stud if she does not have puppies the first time. In some cases the owner of the stud will agree to take a choice puppy in place of the stud fee. You and the owner of the stud should settle all details beforehand, including such questions as what age the puppies should reach before the

Maintenance of a state of excellent health is essential if you are contemplating breeding your bitch or stud. Poor health may not only interfere with reproductive processes but can actually rob your dog of his or her interest in mating. If you are not confident in commercial preparations, consult your vet for the best vitamin supplements to add to your dog's diet.

stud's owner can make his choice, what disposition is made of the single surviving puppy under an agreement by which the stud owner has the pick of the litter, and so on. In all cases, it is best that all agreements entered into by bitch owner and stud owner be in the form of a written contract.

It is customary for the female to be sent to the male. If the stud dog of your choice lives any distance from you, you will have to make arrangements to have your female shipped to him. The quickest way is by air, and if you call your nearest airport the airline people will give you information as to the best and fastest flight. Some airlines furnish their own crates for shipping, whereas others require that you furnish your own. The owner of the stud will make the arrangements for shipping the female back to you. You have to pay all shipping charges.

PREPARATION FOR BREEDING

Before you breed your female, make sure she is in good health. She should be neither too thin nor too fat. Skin diseases must be cured before breeding; a bitch with skin diseases can pass them on to her puppies. If

Perpetual Whelping Chart

	1	2	3	4	5	6	7	8	9	10	11	12	13	14	15	16	17	18	19	20	21	22	23	24	25	26	27	28	29	30	31
Bred—Jan.	1	2	3	4	5	6	7	8	9	10	11	12	13	14	15	16	17	18	19	20	21	22	23	24	25	26	27	28	29	30	31
Due—March	5	6	7	8	9	10	11	12	13	14	15	16	17	18	19	20	21	22	23	24	25	26	27	28	29	30	31	April 1	2	3	4
Bred—Feb.	1	2	3	4	5	6	7	8	9	10	11	12	13	14	15	16	17	18	19	20	21	22	23	24	25	26	27	28			
Due—April	5	6	7	8	9	10	11	12	13	14	15	16	17	18	19	20	21	22	23	24	25	26	27	28	29	30	May 1	2			
Bred—Mar.	1	2	3	4	5	6	7	8	9	10	11	12	13	14	15	16	17	18	19	20	21	22	23	24	25	26	27	28	29	30	31
Due—May	3	4	5	6	7	8	9	10	11	12	13	14	15	16	17	18	19	20	21	22	23	24	25	26	27	28	29	30	31	June 1	2
Bred—Apr.	1	2	3	4	5	6	7	8	9	10	11	12	13	14	15	16	17	18	19	20	21	22	23	24	25	26	27	28	29	30	
Due—June	3	4	5	6	7	8	9	10	11	12	13	14	15	16	17	18	19	20	21	22	23	24	25	26	27	28	29	30	July 1	2	
Bred—May	1	2	3	4	5	6	7	8	9	10	11	12	13	14	15	16	17	18	19	20	21	22	23	24	25	26	27	28	29	30	31
Due—July	3	4	5	6	7	8	9	10	11	12	13	14	15	16	17	18	19	20	21	22	23	24	25	26	27	28	29	30	31	August 1	2
Bred—June	1	2	3	4	5	6	7	8	9	10	11	12	13	14	15	16	17	18	19	20	21	22	23	24	25	26	27	28	29	30	
Due—August	3	4	5	6	7	8	9	10	11	12	13	14	15	16	17	18	19	20	21	22	23	24	25	26	27	28	29	30	31	Sept. 1	
Bred—July	1	2	3	4	5	6	7	8	9	10	11	12	13	14	15	16	17	18	19	20	21	22	23	24	25	26	27	28	29	30	31
Due—September	2	3	4	5	6	7	8	9	10	11	12	13	14	15	16	17	18	19	20	21	22	23	24	25	26	27	28	29	30	Oct. 1	2
Bred—Aug.	1	2	3	4	5	6	7	8	9	10	11	12	13	14	15	16	17	18	19	20	21	22	23	24	25	26	27	28	29	30	31
Due—October	3	4	5	6	7	8	9	10	11	12	13	14	15	16	17	18	19	20	21	22	23	24	25	26	27	28	29	30	31	Nov. 1	2
Bred—Sept.	1	2	3	4	5	6	7	8	9	10	11	12	13	14	15	16	17	18	19	20	21	22	23	24	25	26	27	28	29	30	
Due—November	3	4	5	6	7	8	9	10	11	12	13	14	15	16	17	18	19	20	21	22	23	24	25	26	27	28	29	30	Dec. 1	2	
Bred—Oct.	1	2	3	4	5	6	7	8	9	10	11	12	13	14	15	16	17	18	19	20	21	22	23	24	25	26	27	28	29	30	31
Due—December	3	4	5	6	7	8	9	10	11	12	13	14	15	16	17	18	19	20	21	22	23	24	25	26	27	28	29	30	31	Jan. 1	2
Bred—Nov.	1	2	3	4	5	6	7	8	9	10	11	12	13	14	15	16	17	18	19	20	21	22	23	24	25	26	27	28	29	30	
Due—January	3	4	5	6	7	8	9	10	11	12	13	14	15	16	17	18	19	20	21	22	23	24	25	26	27	28	29	30	31	Feb. 1	
Bred—Dec.	1	2	3	4	5	6	7	8	9	10	11	12	13	14	15	16	17	18	19	20	21	22	23	24	25	26	27	28	29	30	31
Due—February	2	3	4	5	6	7	8	9	10	11	12	13	14	15	16	17	18	19	20	21	22	23	24	25	26	27	28	March 1	2	3	4

she has worms she should be wormed before being bred, or within three weeks afterward. It is a good idea to have your veterinarian give her a booster shot for distemper and hepatitis before the puppies are born. This will increase the immunity the puppies receive during their early, most vulnerable period. Choose a dependable veterinarian and rely on him if there is an emergency when your female whelps.

Do not breed your bitch after she reaches six years of age. If you wish to breed her several times while she is young, it is wise to breed her only once a year. In other words, breed her, skip at least one season, and then breed her again. This will allow her to gain back her full strength between whelpings.

THE IMPORTANCE AND APPLICATION OF GENETICS

Any person attempting to breed dogs should have a basic understanding of the transmission of traits, or characteristics, from the parents to the offspring and some familiarity with the more widely used genetic terms that he will probably encounter. A knowledge of the fundamental mechanics of genetics enables a breeder to better comprehend the passing on of good traits and bad from generation to generation and how a stud and bitch either complement or detract from each other's traits. It enables him to make a more judicial and scientific decision in selecting potential mates.

Inheritance, fundamentally, is due to the existence of microscopic units, known as *GENES,* present in the cells of all individuals. Genes somehow control the biochemical reactions that occur within the embryo or adult organism. This control results in changing or guiding the development of the organism's characteristics. A "string" of attached genes is known as a *CHROMOSOME.* With a few important exceptions, every chromosome has a partner chromosome carrying a duplicate or equivalent set of genes. Each gene, therefore, has a partner gene, known as an *ALLELE.* The number of different pairs of chromosomes present in the cells of the organism varies with the type of organism; a certain parasitic worm has only one pair, a certain fruit fly has four different pairs, man has 23 different pairs and your dog has 39 different pairs per cell. Because each chromosome may have many hundreds of genes, a single cell of the body may contain a total of several thousand genes. Heredity is obviously a very complex matter.

In the simplest form of genetic inheritance, one particular gene and its duplicate, or allele, on the partner chromosome control a single characteristic. The presence of freckles in the human skin, for example, is believed to be due to the influence of a single pair of genes.

Each cell of the body contains the specific number of paired

FERTILIZATION

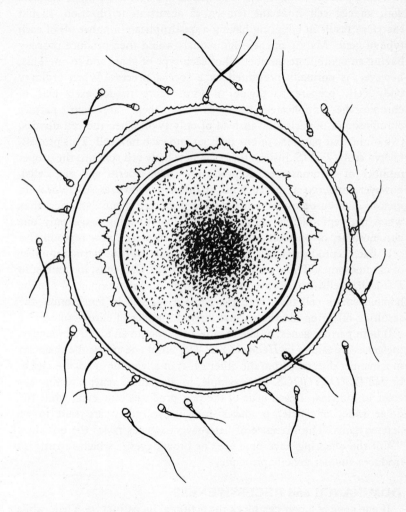

An egg, a special giant cell which the female ovaries produce, is being assaulted by sperm which are attempting to pierce the outer layer of the cell. Only one sperm cell penetration is necessary for fertilization. The first sperm to enter and reach the nucleus will bring with it the necessary chromosomes which will unite with those of the egg. With this union, the full complement of chromosomes necessary for the creation of a new fetus is complete. No other sperm cells are now able to penetrate the egg.

chromosomes characteristic of the organism. Because each type of gene is present on both chromosomes of a chromosome pair, each type of gene is therefore present in duplicate. The fusion of a sperm cell from the male with an egg cell from the female, as occurs in fertilization, should therefore result in offspring having a quadruplicate number (4) of each type of gene. Mating of these individuals would then produce progeny having an octuplicate number (8) of each type of gene, and so on. This, however, is normally prevented by a special process. When ordinary body cells prepare to divide to form more tissue, each pair of chromosomes duplicates itself so that there are four partner chromosomes of each kind instead of only two. When the cell divides, two of the four partners, or one pair, go into each new cell. This process, known as *MITOSIS,* insures that each new body cell contains the proper number of chromosomes. Reproductive cells (sperm and egg cells), however, undergo a special kind of division known as *MEIOSIS.* In meiosis, the chromosome pairs do not duplicate themselves, and thus when the reproductive cells reach the final dividing stage only one chromosome, or one-half of the pair, goes into each new reproductive cell. Each reproductive cell, therefore, has only half the normal number of chromosomes. These are referred to as *HAPLOID* cells, in contrast to *DIPLOID* cells, which have the full number of chromosomes. When the haploid sperm cell fuses with the haploid egg cell in fertilization, the resulting offspring has the normal diploid number of chromosomes.

If both partner genes, or alleles, affect the trait in an identical manner, the genes are said to be *HOMOZYGOUS,* but if one affects the character in a manner different from the other gene, or allele, the genes are said to be *HETEROZYGOUS.* For example, in the pair of genes affecting eye color in humans, if each gene of the pair produces blue eyes, while the other gene, or allele, produces brown eyes, they are said to be heterozygous. The presence of heterozygous genes raises the question, "Will the offspring have blue eyes or brown eyes?" which in turn introduces another genetic principle.

DOMINANCE and RECESSIVENESS

If one gene of a pair can block the action of its partner, or allele, while still producing its own effect, that gene is said to be dominant over its allele. Its allele, on the other hand, is said to be recessive. In the case of heterozygous genes for eye color, the brown eye gene is dominant over the recessive blue eye gene, and the offspring therefore will have brown eyes. Much less common is the occurrence of gene pairs in which neither gene is completely dominant over the other. This, known as IN-COMPLETE or PARTIAL DOMINANCE, results in a blending of the

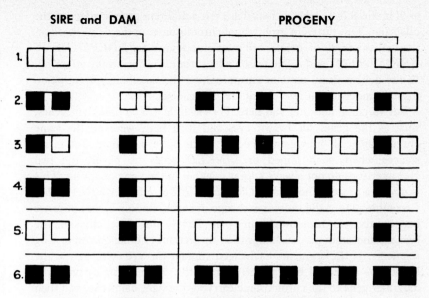

MENDELIAN EXPECTATION CHART

Pictured are the six possible ways in which a pair of genes can unite. The white boxes represent dominant genes; the black boxes represent recessives. Half of the genes of the sire will unite with half of the genes of the dam, and the expected results of such a mating are shown in the progeny combinations. Ratios apply to expectancy over large litters, except in lines 1, 2 and 6 where expectancy is realized in every litter (the exception due to mutation).

opposing influences. In cattle, if a homozygous (pure) red bull is mated with a homozygous (pure) white cow, the calf will be roan, a blending of red and white hairs in its coat, rather than either all red or all white.

During meiosis, or division of the reproductive (sperm and egg) cells, each pair of chromosomes splits, and one-half of each pair goes into one of the two new cells. Thus, in the case of eye color genes, one new reproductive cell will get the chromosome carrying the blue eye gene, while the other new reproductive cell will get the chromosome carrying the brown eye gene, and so on for each pair of chromosomes. If an organism has only one pair of chromosomes—called pair A, made up of chromosomes A_1 and A_2, and pair B, made up of chromosomes B_1 and B_2—each new reproductive cell will get one chromosome from each pair, and four different combinations are possible: A_1 and B_1; A_1 and B_2; A_2 and B_1; or A_2 and B_2. If the blue eye gene is on A_1, the brown eye gene on A_2, and the gene for curly hair on B_1, and the gene for straight hair on B_2, each of the above combinations will exert a different genetic effect on the offspring. This different grouping of chromosomes in the new reproductive cell as a result of meiotic cell division is known as *INDEPENDENT ASSORTMENT* and is one reason why variation occurs in the offspring. In the dog, with 39 pairs of chromosomes, the possibilites of variation through independent assortment are tremendous.

But variation does not end here. For example, if two dominant genes, such as the genes for brown eyes and dark hair, were on the same chromosome, all brown-eyed people would have dark hair. Yet in instances where such joined or *LINKED* genes do occur, the two characteristics do not always appear together in the same offspring. This is due to a process known as a *CROSS-OVER* or *RECOMBINATION*. Recombination is the mutual exchange of corresponding blocks of genes between the two chromosomes in a pair. That is, during cell division, the two chromosomes may exchange their tip sections or other corresponding segments. If the segments exchanged contain the eye color genes, the brown eye gene will be transferred from the chromosome carrying the dark hair gene to the chromosome carrying the light hair gene, and then brown eyes will occur with light hair, provided that the individual is homozygous for the recessive light hair gene.

Another important source of variation is *MUTATION*. In mutation, a gene becomes altered, such as by exposure to irradiation, and exerts a different effect than it did before. Most mutations are harmful to the organism, and some may result in death. Offspring carrying mutated genes and showing the effects of these mutations are known as *MUTANTS* or *SPORTS*. Mutation also means that instead of only two alleles for eye color, such as brown and blue, there may now be three or more (gray, black, etc.) creating a much larger source for possible variation in the offspring.

Further complications in the transmission and appearance of genetic traits are the phenomena known as *EPISTATIS* and *PLEIOTROPY*. Epistatis refers to a gene exerting influence on genes other than its own allele. In all-white red-eyed (albino) guinea pigs, for example, the gene controlling intensity of color is epistatic to any other color gene and prevents that gene from producing its effect. Thus, even if a gene for red spots were present in the cells of the guinea pig, the color intensity gene would prevent the red spots from appearing in the guinea pig's white coat. *Pleiotropy* refers to the fact that a single gene may control a number of characteristics. In the fruit fly, for example, the gene that controls eye color may also affect the structure of certain body parts and even the lifespan of the insect.

One special pair of chromosomes is known as the sex chromosomes. In man, dog, and other mammals, these chromosomes are of two types, designated as X and Y. Under normal conditions, a mammal carrying one X-type and one Y-type is a male. Females have two X chromosomes and can only contribute X chromosomes to the offspring, but the male can contribute either an X or a Y.

If the male's sperm carrying an X chromosome fertilizes the female's egg cell (X), the offspring (XX) will be a female; if a sperm carrying a Y chromosome fertilizes the egg (X), the offspring (XY) will be male. It is the male, therefore, that determines the sex of the offspring in mammals.

Traits controlled by genes present on the sex chromosome, and which appear in only one sex, are said to be *SEX LINKED*. If, for example, a rare recessive gene occurs on the X chromosome, it cannot exert its effect in the female because the dominant allele on the other X chromosomes will counteract it. In the male, however, there is no second X chromosome, and if the Y chromosome cannot offer any countereffect, the recessive character will appear. There are also *SEX-LIMITED* characteristics: these appear primarily or solely in one sex, but the genes for these traits are not carried on the sex chromosomes. Sex-limited traits appear when genes on other chromosomes exert their effect in the proper hormonal (male or female) environment. Sex-linked and sex-limited transmission is how a trait may skip a generation, by being passed from grandfather to grandson through a mother in which the trait, though present, does not show.

In dealing with the simplest form of heredity—one gene effecting one character—there is an expected ratio of the offspring displaying the character to those who do not display it, depending upon the genetic makeup of the parents. If a parent is homozygous for a character, such as blue eyes, it makes no difference which half of the chromosome pair enters the new reproductive cell, because each chromosome carries the gene for blue eyes. If a parent is heterozygous, however, one reproductive cell will receive the brown eye gene while the other will receive the blue eye gene. If both parents are homozygous for blue eyes, all the offspring will receive two blue eye genes, and all will have blue eyes. If a parent is homozygous for blue eyes, and the other parent is homozygous for brown eyes, all the offspring will be heterozygous, receiving one brown eye and one blue eye gene, and because brown is dominant, all will have brown eyes. If both parents are heterozygous, both the blue eye gene and the brown eye gene from one parent have an equal likelihood of ending up with either the blue eye or the brown eye gene from the other parent. This results in a ratio of two heterozygous offspring to the one homozygous for brown eyes and one homozygous for blue eyes, giving a total genetic, or genotypic, ratio of 2:1:1 or, as it is more commonly arranged, 1:2:1. As the two heterozygous as well as the homozygous brown eye offspring will have brown eyes, the ratio of brown eyes to blue eyes (or phenotypic ratio) will be 3:1.

If one parent is heterozygous and the other parent is homozygous for the recessive gene for blue eyes, but the other half of the offspring will be heterozygous and have brown eyes. (Here both the genotypic and phenotypic ratio is 1:1.)

If the homozygous parent, however, has the dominant gene (brown eyes), half of the offspring will be heterozygous and half will be homozygous, as before, but all will have brown eyes. By repeated determinations of these ratios in the offspring, geneticists are able to analyze the genetic makeup of the parents.

Before leaving heredity, it might be well to explain the difference between inbreeding, outcrossing, line breeding, and similar terms. Basically, there are only inbreeding and outbreeding. Inbreeding, however, according to its intensity, is usually divided into interbreeding proper and line breeding. Inbreeding proper is considered to be the mating of very closely related individuals, generally within the immediate family, but this is sometimes extended to include matings to first cousins and grandparents. Line breeding is the mating of more distantly related animals, that is, animals not immediately related to each other but having a common ancestor, such as the same grandsire or great-grandsire. Outbreeding is divided into outcrossing, which is the mating of dogs from different families within the same breed, and cross-breeding, which is mating purebred dogs from different breeds.

From the foregoing discussion of genetics, it should be realized that the theory of telegony, which states that the sire of one litter can influence future litters sired by other studs, is simply not true; it is possible, however, if several males mate with a female during a single estrus cycle, that the various puppies in the litter may have different sires (but not two sires for any one puppy). It should also be realized that blood does not really enter into the transmission of inheritance, although people commonly speak of "bloodlines," "pure-blooded," etc.

7. CARE OF THE MOTHER AND THE NEW FAMILY

PRENATAL CARE OF THE FEMALE

You can expect the puppies nine weeks from the day of breeding, although 58 days is as common as 63. During this time the female should receive normal care and exercise. If she is overweight, don't increase her food at first; excess weight at whelping time is not good. If she is on the thin side, build her up, giving her a morning meal of cereal and egg yolk. Consult your veterinarian as to increasing her vitamins and mineral supplement. During the last weeks the puppies grow enormously, and the mother will have little room for food and less appetite. Divide her meals into smaller portions and feed her more often. If she loses her appetite, tempt her with meat, liver, chicken, etc.

As she grows heavier, eliminate violent exercise and jumping. Do not eliminate exercise entirely, as walking is beneficial to the female in whelp, and mild exercise will maintain her muscle tone in preparation for the birth. Weigh your female after breeding and keep a record of her weight each week thereafter. Groom your bitch daily—some females have a slight discharge during gestation, more prevalent during the last two weeks, so wash the vulva with warm water daily. Usually, by the end of the fifth week you can notice a broadening across her loins, and her breasts become firmer. By the end of the sixth week your veterinarian can tell you whether or not she is pregnant.

PREPARATION OF WHELPING QUARTERS

Prepare a whelping box a few days before the puppies are due, and allow the mother to sleep there overnight or to spend some time in it during the day to become accustomed to it. Then she is less likely to try to have her pups under the front porch or in the middle of your bed. The box should have a wooden floor. Sides about a foot high will keep the puppies in but enable the mother to get out after she has fed them. If the weather is cold, the box should be raised about an inch off the floor.

You should place a guard rail in the whelping box to prevent the mother from rolling over onto the pups and smothering them. This guard is a strip of wood which will project out and above the floor of the box, keeping the bitch from pressing up against the sides of the box.

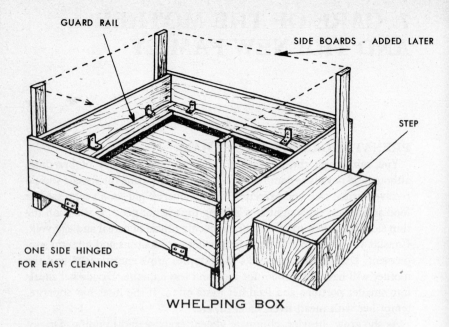

GUARD RAIL

SIDE BOARDS · ADDED LATER

STEP

ONE SIDE HINGED
FOR EASY CLEANING

WHELPING BOX

Layers of newspaper spread over the whole area will make excellent bedding and be absorbent enough to keep the surface warm and dry. They should be removed daily and replaced with another thick layer. An old quilt or washable blanket makes better footing for the nursing puppies than slippery newspaper during the first week, and is softer for the mother. The quilt should be secured firmly.

SUPPLIES TO HAVE ON HAND

As soon as you have the whelping box prepared, set up the nursery by collecting the various supplies you will need when the puppies arrive. You should have the following items on hand: a box lined with towels for the puppies, a heating pad or hot water bottle to keep the puppy box warm, a pile of clean terrycloth towels or washcloths to remove membranes and to dry puppies, a stack of folded newspapers, a roll of paper towels, vaseline, rubber gloves, soap, iodine, muzzle, cotton balls, a small pair of blunt scissors to cut umbilical cords (place scissors into an open bottle of alcohol so they keep freshly sterilized), a rectal thermometer, white thread, a flashlight in case the electricity goes off, a waste container, and a scale for weighing each puppy at birth.

It is necessary that the whelping room be warm and free from drafts, because puppies are delivered wet from the mother. Keep a little notebook and pencil handy so you can record the duration of the first labor and the time between the arrival of each puppy. If there is trouble in whelping, this is the information that the veterinarian will want. Keep his telephone number handy in case you have to call him in an emergency, and warn him to be prepared for an emergency, should you need him.

WHELPING

Be prepared for the actual whelping several days in advance. Usually the female will tear up papers, try to dig nests, refuse food, and generally act restless and nervous. These may be false alarms; the real test is her temperature, which will drop to below 100°F about twelve hours before whelping. Take her temperature rectally at a set time each day, starting about a week before she is due to whelp. After her temperature goes down, keep her constantly with you or put her in the whelping box and stay in the room with her. She will seem anxious and look to you for reassurance. During the birth, if neccesary, be prepared to remove the membranes covering the puppy's head if the mother fails to do this, for the puppy could smother otherwise.

The mother should start licking the puppy as soon as it is out of the sac, thus drying and stimulating it, but if she does not perform this task you can do it with a rough towel, instead. The afterbirth should follow the birth of each puppy, attached to the puppy by the umbilical cord. Watch to make sure that each is expelled, for retaining this material can cause infection. The mother probably will eat the afterbirth after biting the cord. One or two will not hurt her; they stimulate milk supply as well as labor for remaining puppies. Too many, however, can make her lose her appetite for the food she needs to feed her puppies and regain her strength, so remove the rest of them along with the soiled newspaper, and keep the box dry and clean to relieve her anxiety.

If a puppy does not start breathing, wrap him in a towel, hold him upside down with his head toward the ground, and shake him vigorously. If he still does not breathe, rub his ribs briskly; if this also fails, administer artificial respiration by compressing his ribs about twenty times per minute.

If the mother does not bite the cord, or bites it too close to the body, you should take over the job to prevent an umbilical hernia. Cut the cord a short distance from the body with your blunt scissors. Put a drop of iodine on the end of the cord; it will dry up and fall off in a few days.

The puppies should follow each other at regular intervals, but deliveries can be as short as five minutes or as long as two hours apart. A puppy may be presented backwards; if the mother does not seem to be in trouble, *do not interfere*. But if enough of the puppy is outside the birth canal, use a rough towel and help her by pulling gently on the puppy.

Pull only when she pushes. A rear-first, or breech birth can cause a puppy to strangle on its own umbilical cord, so don't let the mother struggle too long. Breech birth is quite common.

When you think all the puppies have been whelped, have your veterinarian examine the mother to determine if all the afterbirths have been expelled. He will probably give her an injection to be certain that the uterus is clean, a shot of calcium for prevention of eclampsia, and possibly an injection of penicillin to prevent infection.

CAESAREAN SECTION

Sometimes a Caesarean section is necessary, although very rarely. The operation of removing the pups by cutting into the abdomen and uterus of the bitch is generally safe; however, if the emergency Caesarean section follows a prolonged, exhausting and fruitless labor, the danger to the bitch is substantially increased.

Reasons for resorting to a Caesarean section include: 1. dystocia due to an abnormally large pup, 2. one presenting in such a way that it cannot get out, is blocking the passage and birth of its littermates or is threatening the life of its dam, 3. an abnormal pelvis in the bitch which does not allow passage of the pups (such as a previous pelvic fracture), 4. inertia, 5. long and arduous labor which exhausts the bitch to the point where weakness causes the uterine and abdominal contractions to stop.

Your bitch can be operated on without losing consciousness if your veterinarian selects to operate with a hypnotic and local anesthesia. The local anesthesia is injected, the incision made, and the pups taken from the semi-conscious bitch.

Gas anesthesia is the safest type of general anesthetic for delivering pups; if barbiturate anesthetics are used intravenously, the puppies may be quite effected by these drugs as they pass through the placental barrier.

Regardless of which method is used for the Caesarean section, the patient should be kept in a warm, clean bed after surgery until she recovers from the anesthesia. The pups should not be placed with the dam until she is once again alert. If the pups are also depressed from the anesthetic, artificial respiration may be required. It is imperative that the pups be kept dry and warm following the delivery.

Offer the puppies to their mother one at a time. After she licks a pup, help it to get settled on a teat and observe them carefully. Rarely, the bitch may not accept her puppies, but this may only be a temporary situation. Watch the mother when she goes out to do her duties; her sutures (stitches) should not be subjected to any undue strain. A binder may interfere with emptying several breasts, but aside from this she will behave in a normal manner. The stitches will be removed in about two weeks and she will be as good as new.

In the cases of both normal and Caesarean delivery the female's temperature should be checked twice daily for one week after delivery. A temperature of over 102°F should be reported to your veterinarian and his directions followed to the letter.

ECLAMPSIA

Eclampsia, or "milk fever," is caused by a lowered calcium content of the blood, due to the bitch's depleting her body's calcium reserves for the production of milk. It is a word that has been fearsome in the dog-breeding world for many years. If it occurs after whelping, the puppies and the mother are in severe danger. Help must be given immediately. The female stiffens her legs, has pale gums, and is likely to have minor convulsions. Puppies must be taken from her and calcium and dextrose administered to her intravenously. However, this is a rare thing and the symptoms so obvious, that assuredly the owner's first thought is that something is wrong and that the veterinarian is needed at once. With proper nutrition during gestation and lactation, a lack of calcium is not to be expected. The best preventive medicine is to see that the female is parasite free, in good condition, and properly cared for from the day she is mated.

HOW TO TAKE CARE OF A LARGE LITTER

The size of a litter varies greatly. If your bitch has a large litter she may have trouble feeding all of the puppies. You can help her by preparing an extra puppy box. Leave half the litter with the mother and the other half in a warm place, changing their places at two-hour intervals at first. Later you may change them less frequently, leaving them all together except during the day. Try supplementary feeding, too, as soon as their eyes are open, since at about two weeks they will lap from a dish.

RAISING THE PUPPIES

Hold each puppy to a breast as soon as he is dry, for a good meal without competition. Then he may join his littermates in the basket, out of his mother's way, while she is whelping. Keep a supply of evaporated milk on hand for emergencies, or later weaning. A formula of evaporated milk, corn syrup and a little water with egg yolk should be warmed and fed in a doll or baby bottle if necessary. A supplementary feeding often helps weak pups over the hump. Keep track of birth weights and take weekly readings so you will have an accurate record of the pups' growth and health.

This compartmentalized incubator demonstrates one method of caring for orphaned puppies. Orphaned pups need to be kept warm by artificial means since they do not have their mother to cuddle next to.

After the puppies have arrived, take the mother outside for a walk and drink, and then leave her to take care of them. She will probably not want to stay away more than a minute or two for the first few weeks. Be sure to keep water available at all times, and feed her milk or broth frequently, as she needs liquids to produce milk. To encourage her to eat, offer her the foods she likes best, until she asks to be fed without your tempting her. She will soon develop a ravenous appetite and should have at least two large meals a day, with dry food available in addition.

Prepare a warm place to put the puppies after they are born to keep them dry and help them to a good start in life. Cover an electric heating pad or hot-water bottle with flannel and put it in the bottom of a cardboard box. Set the box near the mother so that she can see her puppies. She will usually allow you to help, but don't take the puppies out of sight, and let her handle things if your interference seems to make her nervous.

Be sure that all of the puppies are getting enough to eat. If the mother sits or stands, instead of lying still to nurse, the probable cause is scratching from the puppies's nails. You can remedy this by clipping them, as you do hers. Manicure scissors will do for these tiny claws.

The puppies should normally be completely weaned at six weeks, although you start to feed them at three weeks. They will find it easier to lap semi-solid food. At four weeks they will eat four meals a day, and soon do without their mother entirely. Start them on mixed dog food, or leave it with them in a dish for self-feeding. Don't leave water with them all the time; at this age everything is to play with and they will use it as a wading pool. They can drink all they need if it is offered several times a day, after meals.

As the puppies grow up the mother will go into the pen only to nurse them, first sitting up and then standing. To dry her up completely, keep the mother away for longer periods, and then completely. The little milk left will be reabsorbed.

AIRING THE PUPPIES

The puppies may be put outside, unless it is too cold, as soon as their eyes are open. They will benefit from the sunlight and the vitamin D it provides. A rubber mat or newspapers underneath will protect them from cold or damp.

WORMING

You can expect a litter of pups to need at least one worming before they are ready to go to new homes, so take a stool sample to your veterinarian at about six weeks of age. Also, the litter should receive their first temporary shots, which are usually distemper-hepatitis-leptospirosis globulin. Today many kennels are advised by veterinarians to administer these preventative shots even earlier than six weeks, and in special cases they may begin right after birth. The puppy derives immunity from his mother's milk during the first twenty-four hours of his life; this immunity lasts for a varying length of time. Some mothers do not offer any immunity to their young at all. Therefore, in a kennel where the exposure rate is high, and many dogs come and go to shows, and disease may easily be brought to the premises, prophylactic treatment must start early. In the average home, where there is one female and one litter, six weeks is the proper time to start this treatment, and it must be repeated every one to two weeks until the puppies are old enough to have their permanent shots.

PUPPY SOCIALIZATION

Animal psychologists, research scientists and people who train dogs to work closely with people, such as trainers of seeing-eye dogs, have found that the first few weeks of a puppy's life is a critical time. The treatment a puppy receives during this stage determines whether he will become a mentally stable, trustworthy dog that likes people and is able to fit into their particular lifestyle. In general, the dog that is to be a reliable show dog or loving pet must be cuddled often, and experience pleasurable associations with people from a very early age. It is the duty of every creditable breeder to be willing to commit the amount of time necessary to socialize his puppies before he decides to breed his bitch. The behavior of his puppies, whether they are show prospects or pets, reflects on the breed and on his kennel name, two very good reasons for giving the puppies the kind of exposure to human companionship that will turn them into desirable adult dogs. This is not to deny heredity, but to stress the importance of human association in the early weeks of a puppy's life.

Some experts feel that the first three weeks of a puppy's life are completely taken up with nursing, sleeping and keeping warm snuggling with his littermates and dam, and that people-geared socialization should begin after these first three weeks. Others feel that it should begin right away, but that the form varies with the age. During the first weeks while the puppy is still gaining strength and weight and until his eyes are open, socialization should consist of simply holding the tiny pup, stroking its back and tummy for a few minutes and then putting it back with its mother. This should take place with each puppy, every day. As the puppy grows older, the time can be lengthened.

When the puppies are old enough to start eating solid foods, you can reinforce the pleasure contact by feeding them by hand. Basic training and developing receptivity to further training when they are older takes place at this point, so when you call them to you for the hand-held food, **always use the same catch phrase. When the puppies are about a month** old it's time to reinforce their sense of self-sufficiency and ease in new surroundings. This will also ease the transition to a new home. Remove the pups from their whelping box, which until now has circumscribed nearly their entire world, and take them to a different scene. The pup with the most adaptable nature is the one who will immediately move about and begin to explore this new setting. Puppies that are frightened and do not relax after a short time in this new environment should be put back with their mates until next time.

When they are six weeks old, puppies can be further disposed to training by putting a collar on them so they will get used to the feeling of it. Then put on the leash, not to take them for a walk, but just to let them run around in it so they get used to the idea. Later, more serious training can take place by the new owner with the puppy that is taking his place as a temperamentally sound, self-assured, friendly youngster in the world of his human companions.

8. GENERAL HEALTH CARE

WATCHING YOUR PUPPY'S HEALTH

First, don't be frightened by the number of diseases a dog can contract. The majority of dogs never get any of them. Don't become a dog-hypochondriac. All dogs have days when they feel lazy and want to lie around doing nothing. For the few diseases that you might be concerned about, remember that your veterinarian is your dog's best friend. When you first get your puppy, select a veterinarian whom you have faith in. He will get to know your dog and will be glad to have you consult him for advice. A dog needs little medical care, but that little is essential to his good health and well-being. He needs:

1. Proper diet at regular hours
2. Clean, roomy housing
3. Daily exercise
4. Companionship and love
5. Frequent grooming
6. Regular check-ups by your veterinarian

THE USEFUL THERMOMETER

Almost every serious ailment shows itself by an increase in the dog's body temperature. If your dog acts lifeless, looks dull-eyed, and gives the impression of illness, check his temperature by using a rectal thermometer. A stubby end rectal thermometer of either plastic or glass is best suited for this procedure. Although uncommon, there is always the hazard of possible breakage should he become excited during insertion. However, he is easily calmed if you soothe him when the routine is taking place. Hold the dog securely, and insert the thermometer, which you have lubricated with vaseline, and take a reading. The average normal temperature for your dog will be 101.5°F. Excitement may raise the temperature slightly, but any rise of more than a few points is cause for alarm, and your vet should be consulted.

EMERGENCY FIRST AID

In general, a dog will heal his wounds by licking them. If he swallows anything harmful, chances are that he will throw it up. But it will probably make you feel better to help him if he is hurt, so treat his wounds as you would your own. Wash out the dirt and apply an antiseptic.

If you fear that your dog has swallowed poison, get him to the veterinarian's *at once*. In the meantime, try and locate the source of poisoning; if he has swallowed, for example, a cleaning fluid kept in your house, check the bottle label to see if inducing the dog to vomit is necessary. In some cases, inducing the dog to vomit can be very harmful, depending upon the type of poison swallowed. Amateur diagnosis is very dangerous, when you consider that time is so extremely important.

Accidents

Accidents, unfortunately, will happen so it is best to be prepared. If your dog gets hit by a car, keep him absolutely quiet, move him as little as possible and get veterinary treatment as soon as possible. It is unwise to give any stimulants such as brandy or other alcoholic liquids where there is visible external hemorrhage or the possibility of internal hemorrhaging. If your dog has cut his foot or leg badly, on glass or otherwise, bandage the wound as tightly as possible to stop the bleeding. A wad of cotton may serve as a pressure bandage, which will ordinarily stop the flow of blood. Gauze wrapped around the cotton will hold it in place. Usually, applying such pressure to a wound will sufficiently stop the blood flow; however, for severe bleeding, such as when an artery is cut, a tourniquet may be necessary. Apply a tourniquet between the injury and the heart if the bleeding is severe. To tighten the tourniquet, push a pencil through the bandage and twist it. Take your dog to a veterinarian immediately since a tourniquet should not be left in place any longer than fifteen minutes.

Blood coming from an artery is bright red in color and will spurt in unison with the heart beat. From a vein, it is dark red and continuous in flow.

Burns and Scalds

Any dog kept in the home runs the risk of being burned or scalded at one time or another. If your pet sustains a serious burn, call the vet immediately as shock quickly follows such a burn. The dog should be kept warm and quiet, wrapped in a blanket. If he still shows signs of being chilled, use a hot water bottle. Clean the burn gently, removing any foreign matter such as bits of lint, hair, grass or dirt. Act as quickly as possible. Prevent exposure to air by applying olive oil or another similar substance and cover with gauze, cotton and a loose bandage. To prevent the dog from interfering with the dressing, muzzle him and have someone stay with him until veterinary treatment is at hand.

If the burn or scald is a minor one clip hair away from the affected area and apply a paste of bicarbonate of soda and water. Apply it thickly to the burned area and try to keep the dog from licking it off.

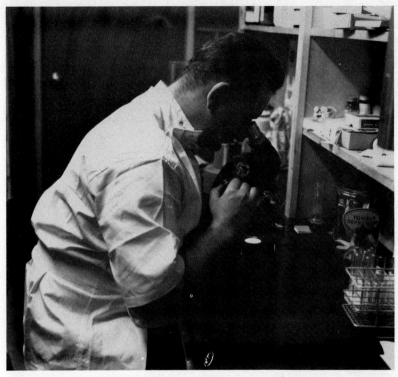

Often the only way to adequately determine the best treatment for your dog is through microscopic analysis of a blood smear or tissue scraping so the veterinarian can diagnose the ailment exactly.

Snake Bite

If your dog is bitten by a poisonous snake, open up the wound with any available instrument that is sharp and clean. Squeeze the wound to cause a fair amount of blood to flow. This will wash the poison from the wound as much as possible. The dog should be taken to the veterinarian immediately so antitoxins can be administered. If the bite has been sustained on the leg, it is advisable to apply a tourniquet if at all possible to keep the poison from flowing further. Under no circumstances should snake bite from a poisonous snake, or its treatment, be taken lightly.

Stings

Many dogs enjoy trying to catch wasps and bees. When these insects are prevalent it is difficult to stop your pet from snapping at them. A sting frequently follows a successful catch and it often occurs inside the mouth, which can be very serious. The best remedy is to get him to a veterinarian as soon as possible, but there are some precautionary measures to follow in the meantime. If the dog has been lucky enough to only be caught on the outside of the face, try to extricate the stinger, then swab the point of entry with a solution of bicarbonate of soda. In the case of a wasp sting, use vinegar or some other acidic food stuff. A useful remedy for wasp stings is to rub the part with moistened tobacco, i.e., an unsmoked cigarette end that has been moistened.

IMPORTANCE OF INOCULATIONS

With the proper series of inoculations, your dog will be almost completely protected against disease. However, it occasionally happens that the shot does not take, and sometimes a different form of the virus appears against which your dog may not be protected.

Distemper

Probably the most virulent of all dog diseases is distemper. Young dogs are most susceptible to it, although it may affect dogs of all ages. The dog will lose his appetite, seem depressed, chilled, and run a fever. Often he will have a watery discharge from his eyes and nose. Unless treated promptly, the disease goes into advanced stages with infections of the lungs, intestines, and nervous system, and dogs that recover may be left with some impairment such as paralysis, convulsions, a twitch, or some other defect, usually spastic in nature. The best protection against this is very early inoculation with a series of permanent shots and a booster shot each year thereafter.

Hepatitis

Veterinarians report an increase in the spread of this viral disease in recent years, usually with younger dogs as the victims. The initial symptoms—drowsiness, vomiting, great thirst, loss of appetite, and a high temperature—closely resemble those of distemper. These symptoms are often accompanied by swellings of the head, neck, and abdomen. The disease strikes quickly; death may occur in just a few hours. Protection is afforded by injection with a vaccine recently developed.

Leptospirosis

This disease is carried by bacteria that live in stagnant or slow-moving water. It is carried by rats and dogs; infection is begun by the dog's licking substances contaminated by the urine or feces of infected animals. The symptoms are diarrhea and a yellowish-brownish discoloration of the jaws, tongue, and teeth, caused by an inflammation of the kidneys.

This disease can be cured if caught in time, but it is best to ward it off with a vaccine which your veterinarian can administer along with the distemper shots.

Rabies

This is an acute disease of the dog's central nervous system. It is spread by infectious saliva transmitted by the bite of an infected animal. Rabies is generally manifested in one of two classes of symptoms. The first is "furious rabies," in which the dog shows a period of melancholy or depression, then irritation, and finally paralysis. The first period lasts from a few hours to several days. During this time the dog is cross and will change his position often. He loses his appetite for food and begins to lick, bite and swallow foreign objects. During the irritative phase the dog is spasmodically wild and has impulses to run away. He acts in a fearless manner and runs at and bites everything in sight. If he is caged or confined he will fight at the bars, often breaking teeth or fracturing his jaw. His bark becomes a peculiar howl. In the final, or paralytic, stage, the animal's lower jaw becomes paralyzed and hangs down; he walks with a stagger and saliva drips from his mouth. Within four to eight days after the onset of paralysis, the dog dies.

The second class of symptoms is referred to as "dumb rabies" and is characterized by the dog's walking in a bearlike manner, head down. The lower jaw is paralyzed and the dog is unable to bite. Outwardly, it may seem as though he had a bone caught in his throat.

Even if your pet should be bitten by a rabid dog or other animal, he probably can be saved if you get him to the veterinarian in time for a series of injections. However, after the symptoms have appeared no cure is possible. But remember that an annual rabies inoculation is almost certain protection against rabies. If you suspect that your dog has rabies, notify your local Health Department. A rabid dog is a danger to all who come near him.

Canine Parvovirus

This highly contagious virus disease has recently joined the ranks of potential canine killers and has spread in almost epidemic proportions throughout certain sections of the United States. It has appeared in Canada, Australia and Europe as well. CPV attacks the intestinal tract, white blood cells, and less frequently the heart muscle. It is believed to spread through dog-to-dog contact, the specific source of infection being the fecal waste matter of infected dogs. CPV is particularly hard to overcome because it is capable of existing in the environment for many months under varying conditions unless strong disinfectants are used.

CPV's high degree of contagion is augmented by the fact that it can readily be transmitted from place to place on the hair and feet of infected dogs. Contact with contaminated cages, shoes, and the like can also transmit CPV. However, while it is highly contagious among dogs, the disease cannot be contracted by other animals or people from infected dogs.

The initial signs of infection of this viral disease are normally vomiting and severe diarrhea, which will appear within five to seven days after the individual has been exposed to the virus. At the onset of illness, feces will be light gray or yellow-gray in color. Occasionally, the dog's diarrheal waste will be blood-streaked. Because of the vomiting and severe diarrhea, the dog that has contracted the disease will dehydrate quickly. Depression and loss of appetite can accompany the other symptoms as well as a rise in temperature in younger dogs especially. Temperatures may range from 104 degrees to 106. Older dogs may suffer no temperature increase at all and generally CPV is fatal in only two to three percent of those afflicted.

Death caused by this disease normally occurs within 48 to 72 hours following the appearance of the symptoms. Puppies are hardest hit, with the virus being fatal to 75 percent of puppies that contract it. Death is almost shock-like in their case and can occur within two days of the onset of the illness.

The best preventive measure for CPV is vaccination administered by your veterinarian. Consult him about the duration of immunity of each inoculation and for a schedule of future inoculations. Precautionary measures individual pet owners can take include disinfecting the kennel and other areas where the dog is housed. Since the virus is hardy and capable of existing for many months, a strong disinfectant must be used. One part sodium hypochlorite solution (household bleach), to 30 parts of water will do the job efficiently. Keep the dog from coming into contact with the fecal matter of other dogs when walking or exercising your pet.

HIP DYSPLASIA

This often crippling condition is more prevalent in large breeds than in small, but has occurred in almost every breed. The cause is not absolutely known though it is believed to be hereditary and as yet there is no known cure. The condition exists in varying degrees of severity. In general, hip dysplasia can be described as a poor fit between the two bones of the hip joint—the femur and the acetabulum—and is caused by a malformation of one or the other. Either the head of the femur is flattened causing it to slip out of the socket, or a shallowness of the acetabulum causes the femur to slip out. HD is usually graded according to severity and poorness of fit between the ball and socket, with the lowest grades being the best fit and the higher end of the scale denoting the worst cases.

HD causes stiffness in the hindlegs, considerable pain in the more severe cases and difficulty of movement. It generally manifests itself in puppyhood and can be noticed by the time the young dog is two months old. Severity can usually be determined by the age of six months. If HD is suspected, the dog should be x-rayed, and if afflicted it should not be used for breeding. Cases vary greatly, but severe pain may be more or less continuous in advanced cases. When this is true euthanasia is occasionally recommended, though medication is available to control the pain and allow the dog to move with more ease. Rigorous exercise is not recommended since it only increases the rate at which the bone surfaces wear away.

COUGHS, COLDS, BRONCHITIS, PNEUMONIA

Respiratory diseases may affect the dog because he is forced to live under man-made conditions rather than in his natural environment. Being subjected to cold or a draft after a bath, sleeping near an air conditioner or in the path of a fan or near a radiator can cause respiratory ailments. The symptoms are similar to those in humans. The germs of these diseases, however, are different and do not affect both dogs and humans, so they cannot be infected by each other. Treatment is much the same as for a child with the same type of illness. Keep the dog warm, quiet, and well fed. Your veterinarian has antibiotics and other remedies to help the dog recover.

DIABETES MELLITUS (Sugar Diabetes)

This is a disease wherein the sugar balance of the body is disturbed because of insufficient production of the hormone insulin. The pancreas secretes insulin which regulates carbohydrate/sugar usage. When the insulin-producing cells are damaged, the condition arises. It is marked by an increase in the blood sugar level and an excessive amount of sugar is excreted in the urine.

Symptoms of the condition are great thirst, increased urination and loss of weight while the appetite and food consumption increases. The signs vary in severity. If overlooked, emaciation and collapse rapidly occur. The dog can go into a diabetic coma and die.

Treatment is the same as for human diabetes, utilizing dietary regulation and insulin injections if necessary. The diet should be one of very low fat, with a low percentage of carbohydrate and a higher pecentage of protein. The insulin dose must be adjusted as indicated by urine tests which your veterinarian can teach you to administer at home. The test makes use of chemically treated sticks, pale yellow in color, which turn to various shades of green when dipped in urine. The darker the shade, the more serious the condition.

INTERNAL PARASITES

There are four common internal parasites that may infect your dog. These are roundworms, hookworms, whipworms, and tapeworms. The first three can be diagnosed by laboratory examination; the presence of tapeworms is determined by seeing segments in the stool or attached to the hair around the tail. Do not under any circumstances attempt to worm your dog without the advice of your veterinarian. After first determining what type of worm or worms are present, he will advise you of the best method of treatment.

A dog or puppy in good physical condition is less susceptible to worm infestation than a weak dog. Proper sanitation and a nutritious diet help in preventing worms. One of the best preventative measures is to always have clean, dry bedding for your dog. This will diminish the possibility of reinfection due to flea or tick bites.

Heartworms

Heartworm infestation in dogs is passed by mosquitoes and can be a life threatening problem. Dogs with the disease tire easily, have difficulty breathing, cough and may lose weight despite a hearty appetite. If caught in the early stages, the disease can be effectively treated; however, the administration of daily preventative medicine throughout the spring, summer and fall months is strongly advised. Your veterinarian must first take

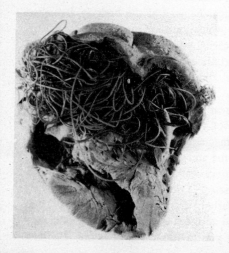

Pictured is the heart of a dog showing a heavy infestation of heartworms. Mosquitoes carry the offspring of the adult worms which are implanted into a dog's bloodstream when the dog is bitten. The worm offspring travel to the heart where they do their damage as they develop into adult worms. U.S.D.A.

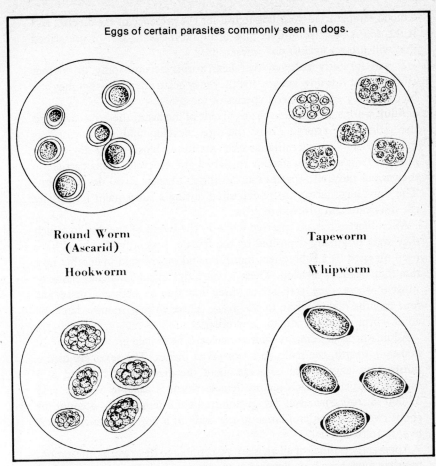

Eggs of certain parasites commonly seen in dogs.

Round Worm
(Ascarid)

Hookworm

Tapeworm

Whipworm

The presence of worms in your dog's system can manifest itself in outward signs such as a general deterioration, loss of weight, dulling of coat, diarrhea and vomiting. *Roundworm* larvae penetrate the intestinal lining, where they enter the bloodstream and are carried to the lungs. This worm affects mostly puppies, in whom it can cause lung damage and intestinal blockage. There are many species of *tapeworm* that can infest your dog. The important factor in breaking the life cycle of the tapeworm is the elimination of the parasitic host on which the worm thrives. Fleas are perhaps the most common host, so ridding your dog of them is a step toward eliminating the possibility of tapeworm infection. If present in massive quantities, *hookworms*, which remove blood from the dog, may cause circulatory collapse and ultimate death. *Whipworms* may cause weight loss, vomiting, diarrhea and secondary anemia in an affected dog.

a blood sample from your dog to test for the presence of the disease, and if the dog is heartworm-free, pills or liquid medicine can be prescribed that will protect against any infestation.

It was formerly believed that heartworms occured only in warmer climates, but it is now known that they may occur anywhere that they can be carried by any of several species of mosquitoes.

Adult worms are found in the right side of the heart, the vena cavae and the pulmonary artery. There the eggs develop and are released as microfilariae. The microfilariae circulate in the blood of the dog until a mosquito ingests them, starting the larval growth cycle. Being carried by the various mosquito species induces the third-stage larval development. The third-stage larvae are re-deposited during a subsequent feeding by the mosquito and proceed to grow.

Microfilariae remain inactive while in the blood of the dog in which they were originally deposited by the female. It is only after they have been ingested by a subsequent mosquito and redeposited in another host that they begin to develop. These larvae lodge in subcutaneous tissue or muscle where they stay about three months; at between three and four months they migrate to the heart. Three to four months later the adult worm begins producing microfilariae.

Adult worms are creamy white in color. The female grows to 11 or 12 inches in length, the male, to six or seven inches. The sexes are distinquished by length since both are about the diameter of the lead in a mechanical pencil. Each mature female worm is capable of producing 30,000 microfilariae each day. A hundred adult females can account for about two billion microfilariae in the body of a dog since microfilariae live up to two years.

Apparently canines of all ages are susceptible to heartworm infestation, but they must have been exposed to mosquitoes in order to have acquired the third-stage infective larvae. Heartworm infection increases markedly as the dog matures. If left undetected, it will erode the heart.

A microscopic search for microfilariae is necessary to prove that adult worms are present. Because of the large number and size of the worms, treatment must be careful and slow to minimize damage to the circulatory system.

SKIN AILMENTS

Any persistent scratching may indicate an irritation. Whenever you groom your dog, look for the reddish spots that may indicate eczema, mange, or fungal infection. Rather than treating your dog yourself, take him to the veterinarian, as some of the conditions may be difficult to eradicate and can cause permanent damage to his coat.

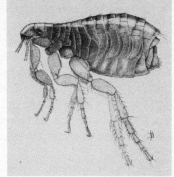

Two of the most common external parasites are the tick (left) and the flea (right). Along with the general discomfort and irritation that they bring to your dog, these parasites can infest him with worms and disease. The flea is a carrier of tapeworm, and may act as an intermediate host for heartworm. The tick can cause dermatitis and anemia in your dog, and may also be a carrier of Rocky Mountain spotted fever and canine babesiasis, a blood infection.

External Parasites

The dog that is groomed regularly and provided with clean sleeping quarters should not be troubled by fleas, ticks, or lice. If the dog should become infested with any of these parasites, he should be treated with medicated dip bath or the new oral medications that are presently available.

Mange

There are two types of mange, sarcoptic and follicular, both of which are caused by a parasite. The former is by far the more common, and results in an intense irritation, causing violent scratching. Close examination will reveal small red spots which become filled with pus. This is a highly contagious condition, and any dog showing signs of the disease should be isolated. Consult your veterinarian for the proper treatment procedures. Follicular mange is very much harder to cure, but fortunately, it is much rarer and less contagious. This disease will manifest itself as bare patches appearing on the skin, which becomes thickened and leathery. A complete cure from this condition is only rarely effected.

Eczema

This disease occurs most often in the summer months and affects the dog down the back, especially just above the root of the tail. It should not be confused with mange, as it is not caused by a parasite. One of the principle causes of eczema is improper nutrition, which makes the dog susceptible to disease. Hot, humid weather predisposes the growth of bacteria, which can invade a susceptible dog and thereby cause skin irritations and lesions. It is imperative that the dog gets relief from the itching that is symptomatic of the disease as this self-mutilation by scratching will only help to spread the inflammation. Antibiotics may be necessary if a bacterial infection is, indeed, present. The dog must be thoroughly ridded of fleas to avoid any recurrance of the scratching that can spread the disease.

Moist eczema, commonly referred to as "hot spots," is a rapidly appearing skin disease that produces a moist infection. Spots appear very suddenly and may spread rapidly in a few hours, infecting several parts of the body. These lesions are generally bacterially infected and are extremely itchy, which will cause the dog to scratch frantically and further damage the afflicted areas. Vomiting, fever and an enlargement of the lymph nodes may occur. The infected areas must be clipped to the skin and thoroughly cleaned. Your veterinarian will prescribe an anti-inflammatory drug and antibiotics, as well as a soothing emollient to relieve itching.

EYES, EARS, TEETH AND NAILS

If your dog is to remain in good health, you must be aware of the need for periodic "examinations" in which you routinely inspect him for unusual signs of irritation or infection. In most cases, the tell-tale warning signals are any unusual swelling, discharge or redness that may appear, especially after an injury.

The eyes, because of their sensitivity, are prone to injury and infection. Dogs that spend a great deal of time outdoors in heavily wooded areas may return from an exercise excursion with watery eyes, the result of brambles and high weeds scratching them. The eyes may also be irritated by dirt and other foreign matter.

Should your dog's eyes appear red and watery, a mild solution can be mixed at home for a soothing washing. Your veterinarian will be able to tell you what percentage of boric acid, salt, or other medicinal compound to mix with water.

You must monitor your dog's eyes after such a solution is administered; if the irritation persists, or if there is a significant discharge, immediate veterinary attention is warranted.

Your dog's ears, like his eyes, are extremely sensitive and can also be prone to infection, should wax and/or dirt be allowed to build up. Ear irritants may be present in the form of mites, soap or water, or foreign par-

The Elizabethan collar is designed to keep your dog from scratching the area about his head and ears when a wound or sutures there advise against scratching. While they can be purchased ready-made, they can also be easily made at home from a piece of cardboard box. Be sure the hole is large enough so that it does not constrict the dog's breathing or swallowing.

ticles which the dog has come into contact with while romping through a wooded area. If your dog's ears are bothering him, you will know it—he will scratch and paw them, shake his head, and the ears will show a foul-smelling dark secretion. This pasty secretion usually signals the onset of *otorrhea*, or ear canker, and at this stage proper veterinary care is essential if the dog's hearing is not to be permanently impaired. In the advanced stages of ear canker, tissue builds up within the ear, and the ear canal becomes blocked off, thus eliminating the hearing abilities of that ear.

If this is to be prevented, you should wash your dog's ears as they require it, with a very dilute solution of hydrogen peroxide and water, or an antibacterial ointment, as your vet suggests. In any case, the ears, because of their delicacy, are to be washed gently, with a soft cloth or cotton.

The good health of your pet's teeth can be maintained by his regular use of a chew product such as Nylabone® or Nylaball®, which serves to clean the teeth of tartar accumulation and massage and stimulate the gums. With puppies, a chew product helps to relieve the discomfort of the teething stage, and of course prevents the pup's chewing of your furniture and slippers!

A periodic inspection of your dog's mouth will alert you to any problem he might have that would require a trip to the veterinarian's office. Any signs of tooth or gum sensitivity, redness or swelling, signal the need for professional treatment. Also, it is best to have your pet's teeth scraped once or twice a year, at the time that he goes to the vet's for his general physical check-up. This simple procedure removes any excess tartar that

Badly decayed teeth can cause abscesses of mouth tissues and gums, and even bone deterioration in extreme cases. Pain caused by such a condition can discourage your dog from eating even though he is hungry, resulting in possible malnutrition or even starvation. Your vet should be consulted if any listlessness or change in eating habits is noticed.

Dog nail clippers are designed to trim nails quickly and easily with a minimum of scuffling between you and your dog. While other general purpose instruments can be used, there is a greater chance with these of cutting too far down on the nail and hitting the vein, resulting in a painful experience for your dog.

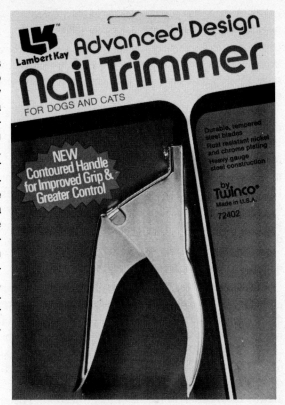

has accumulated on his teeth that could cause degeneration of tooth enamel, if left to build up.

If you live in a city and walk your dog regularly on pavement, chances are that his nails are kept trimmed from the "wear and tear" they receive from the sidewalks. However, if your dog gets all of his exercise in your yard, or if his nails simply grow rather quickly, it will occasionally be necessary for you to clip his nails. It is best for you to have your veterinarian show you the proper way to perform the nail clipping at first. Special care must always be taken to avoid cutting too far and reaching the "quick." If you cut into the quick of the nail, it will bleed, so it is easy to see why an expert must show you the proper procedure. A nail clipper designed especially for dogs can be purchased at any pet shop.

CARE OF THE AGED DOG

With the increased knowledge and care available, there is no reason why your dog should not live to a good old age. As the years go by he may need a little additional care. Remember that an excessively fat dog is not healthy, particularly as he grows older, so limit the older dog's food accordingly. He needs exercise as much as ever, although his heart cannot bear the strain of sudden and violent exertion. Failing eyesight or hearing means lessened awareness of dangers, so you must protect him more than ever.

Should you decide at this time to get a puppy, to avoid being without a dog when your old friend is no longer with you, be very careful how you introduce the puppy. He naturally will be playful and will expect the older dog to respond to his advances. Sometimes the old dog will get a new lease on life from a new puppy, but he may be consumed with jealousy. Do not give the newcomer the attention that formerly was exclusively the older dog's. Feed them apart, and show your old friend that you still love him the most; the puppy, not being accustomed to individual attention, will not mind sharing your love.

TATTOOING

Tattooing is an increasingly popular method of identifying your dog that has met with growing success in assuring the safe return of lost or stolen dogs. Several registries exist that will record a dog's tattoo number along with his owner's name, address and telephone number. Two types of tattoo numbers can be assigned. In the case of mixed breed dogs, the owner's social security number is generally used; in the case of pedigreed dogs, the dog's AKC registration number is used. These two numbers are the most common means of identification. The groin or inside of the ear is the usual spot for the tattoo mark, though cases have been cited in which a dog's ear was cut off to eliminate the possibility of catching the dognappers.

For a minor fee, your veterinarian can do the simple, painless job that may insure the return of a beloved pet or show dog. Such return would be reward enough for the few minutes it takes to have this simple procedure done. Since a puppy grows very rapidly, it is best not to have him tattooed until he is at least four months old to avoid any possible smearing of the tattoo ink. There is almost no danger of infection if the job is done properly and exhibitors run no risk of having the show dog's career impaired by the tattoo mark since the AKC has ruled that no judge may disqualify or penalize a dog because of a tattoo.

Your local kennel club will be able to supply the name of a registry in your area.

9. DOG SHOW COMPETITION

There is no greater pleasure for the owner than showing a beautiful dog perfectly groomed and trained for the show ring. Whether he wins or not, it is gratifying to show a dog in superb condition, one that is a credit to your training and care. A great deal of preparation, both for you and your dog, is needed before the day that you do any serious winning. Showing is not as easy as it looks, even if you have a magnificent dog. He must be presented to the judge so that all of his good points are shown to advantage. This requires practice in gaiting, daily grooming from puppyhood, and the proper diet to make him sound in body.

When you buy your puppy you probably will think he is the best in the country and possibly in the world, but before you enter the highly competitive world of dog shows, get an unbiased expert opinion. Visit a few dog shows as a spectator and make mental notes of what is required of the handlers and dogs. Watch how the experienced handlers manage their dogs to bring out their best points.

HOW TO SELECT A SHOW DOG

If you are planning to show your dog, it is best not to buy a puppy any younger than four or six months of age. Since it is difficult at best to predict what a puppy will look like at maturity, you cannot rely wholly on its appearance while it is only six or eight weeks old. By doing a certain amount of homework before purchasing your show dog, you can be assured to an extent that you will end up with a show quality dog that will hold its own in the show rings. Before going out to buy, read some good books on your breed. Consult a reputable book of standards for the breed to get an idea of what the dog should look like as an adult. Remember that no individual dog ever completely achieves the standard, but knowing the important conformational points of the breed will help to illustrate what you are aiming for in your show dog. Attending dog shows and talking with veterans who have been in the dog game for a while will give you valuable information to use when choosing your own show prospect.

One of the best assurances you can get in a field where there are no real guarantees is to search out well-known breeders who are known to have successfully bred show winners through several generations. Ask to look at the pedigree of any puppy you are considering buying, noting whether there are numerous top-quality dogs in the ancestry. Have the sire and

When you purchase your puppy, the breeder can supply you with a pedigree for him. A puppy of champion bloodlines is often of superior quality.

dam of the litter you are interested in been bred before, and if so, what was the overall quality of their previous offspring? If they have produced consistently good dogs through several of the same pairings, your chances of getting a good specimen are fairly high. If the stud or bitch, or both, are unproven in previous litters, the probability of attaining top quality in the puppies is less likely.

In general, the rule of thumb to follow is to go by the expertise of the breeder. A reputable breeder will sell you the best dog possible if you make it clear to him that the dog will definitely be used for a show career. The show contender you purchase not only represents you as its owner, but also reflects the quality of the kennel of the breeder. The reputation of both exhibitor and breeder is made by the quality of the dogs they present, so careful selection of a show dog is essential to all involved.

TYPES OF DOG SHOWS

There are various types of dog shows. The American Kennel Club sanctioned matches are shows at which purebred dogs may compete, but not for championship points. These are excellent for you to enter to accustom you and your dog to showing. If your dog places in a few match shows, then you might seriously consider entering the big-time shows. An American Kennel Club all-breed show is one at which purebred dogs compete for championship points. An American Kennel Club specialty show is for one breed only. It may be held in conjunction with an all-breed show (by designating the classes at that show as its specialty show) or it may be held entirely apart. Obedience trials are different in that in them the dog is judged according to his obedience and ability to perform, not by his conformation to the breed standard.

There are two types of championship conformation shows: *benched* and *unbenched*. At a benched show your dog must be on his appointed bench during the advertised hours of the show's duration. He may be removed from the bench only to be taken to the exercise pen or to be groomed (an hour before the showing) in an area designated for handlers to set up their crates and grooming tables. At an unbenched show your car may serve as a bench for your dog.

To become a champion your dog must win fifteen points in competition with other dogs; a portion of the fifteen points must be awarded as major point wins (three to five points) under different judges.

This scene from a large indoor show captures the exciting moment when the group winners go before the judge for the Best In Show competition.

HOW TO ENTER

If your dog is purebred and registered with the AKC—or eligible for registration—you may enter him in the appropriate show class for which his age, sex, and previous show record qualify him. You will find coming shows listed in the different dog magazines or at your petshop. Write to the secretary of the show, asking for the premium list. When you receive the entry form, fill it in carefully and send it back with the required entry fee. Then, before the show, you should receive your exhibitor's pass, which will admit you and your dog to the show. Here are the five official show classes:

PUPPY CLASS: Open to dogs at least six months and not more than twelve months of age. Limited to dogs whelped in the United States and Canada.

NOVICE CLASS: Open to dogs six months of age or older that have never won a first prize in any class other than puppy class, and less than three first prizes in the novice class itself. Limited to dogs whelped in the United States or Canada.

BRED BY EXHIBITOR CLASS: Open to all dogs, except cham-

To transport your dog long distances, crates should be used that have been made especially for that purpose. They are designed to give your dog optimum ventilation and comfort, while still assuring his maximum safety and protection.

Your pet store carries a large number of pet feeding and watering bowls, in sizes suitable for any size dog. While at a show, be sure to supply your dog with a light meal and some fresh water to keep him comfortable.

pions, six months of age or over which are exhibited by the same person, or his immediate family, or kennel that was the recognized breeder on the records of the American Kennel Club.

AMERICAN-BRED CLASS: Open to dogs that are not champions, six months of age or over, whelped in the United states after a mating which took place in the United States.

OPEN CLASS: Open to dogs six months of age or over, with no exceptions.

In addition there are local classes, the Specials Only class, and brace and team entries.

For full information on dog shows, read the book *How to Show Your Own Dog,* by Virginia Tuck Nichols. (T.F.H.)

JUNIOR SHOWMANSHIP

If you have considered that you and your dog are going to go the show route, you might consider having your youngster show the dog in the ring. If your child has an especially good relationship with his pet, or if he has trained the dog himself, as many children do, then Junior Showmanship might be a good learning experience.

Junior Showmanship is competition among children of different age groups, handling dogs owned by their immediate families. The age divisions are: Novice A, for 10 to 12 year olds; Novice B, for those boys and girls from 13 to 16 (entrants in these two classes must have one or no prior Junior Showmanship wins); Open A for those 10 to 12 years of age; Open B for those 13 to 16 (these entrants must have earned two or more Junior Showmanship awards).

Children involved in JS have the wonderful opportunity to feel a sense of achievement and victory, should they walk away with the ribbons after a show. Even still, winning is not the most important factor here: the pride and responsibility the youngster feels at having reached the ring is surely worth the effort and discipline required to enter showmanship competition.

For more information on JS, and to obtain a rules and regulations booklet, you can contact the American Kennel Club in New York.

ADVANCED PREPARATION

Before you go to a show your dog should be trained to gait at a trot beside you, with head up and in a straight line. In the ring you will have to gait your dog around the edge with other dogs and then individually up and down the center runner. In addition the dog must stand for ex-

If yours is intended to be a show dog, you will want to be prepared with all the tools and equipment necessary for the meticulous grooming of a show dog. Several different types of combs, brushes, clippers and coat grooming products can be obtained from the local pet store.

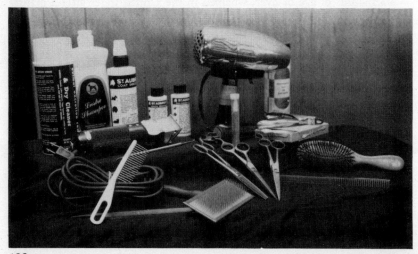

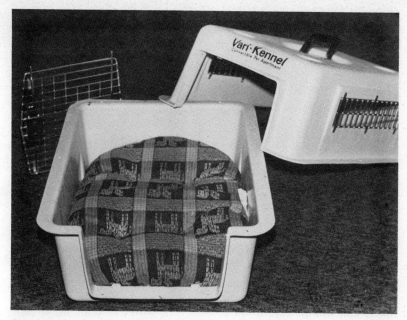

Be sure to take along a comfortable carrier for your dog if he is to be confined, or benched, during the show's duration.

amination by the judge, who will look at him closely and feel his head and body structure. He should be taught to stand squarely, hind feet slightly back, head up on the alert. Showing requires practice training sessions in advance. Get a friend to act as judge and set the dog up and "show" him a few minutes every day.

Sometime before the show, give your dog a bath so he will look his best. Get together all the things you will need to take to the show. You will want to take a water dish and a bottle of water for your dog (so he won't be affected by a change in drinking water). Take your show lead, bench chain (if it is a benched show), combs and brush, and the identification ticket sent by the show superintendent, noting the time you must be there and the place where the show will be held, as well as the time of judging.

THE DAY OF THE SHOW

Don't feed your dog the morning of the show, or give him at most a light meal. He will be more comfortable in the car on the way, and will show more enthusiastically. When you arrive at the show grounds, find out where he is to be benched and settle him there. Your bench or stall

Conformation to the ideal standard for the breed will be recognized in show dogs by the awarding of ribbons and trophies. Dog show entrants can win on several different levels, with the most significant and exciting award being Best In Show honors.

number is on your identification ticket, and the breed name will be on placards fastened to the ends of the row of benches. Once you have your dog securely fastened to his stall by a bench chain (use a bench crate instead of a chain if you prefer), locate the ring where your dog will be judged (the number and time of showing will be on the program of judging which came with your ticket). After this you may want to take your dog to the exercise ring to relieve himself, and give him a small drink of water. Your dog will have been groomed before the show, but give him a final brushing just before going into the show ring. When your breed judging is called, it is your responsibility to be at the ringside ready to go in. The steward will give you an armband which has on it the number of your dog.

Then, as you step into the ring, try to keep your knees from knocking! Concentrate on your dog and before you realize it you'll be out again, perhaps back with the winners of each class for more judging and finally, with luck, it will be over and you'll have a ribbon and trophy—and, of course, the most wonderful dog in the world!

10. BUILDING A KENNEL AND EXERCISE RUNS

DRAWING UP PLANS

Whether you have one dog or many, the time may come when you decide that an outdoor kennel and runs will best satisfy your dog's exercise and housing needs. Properly built and maintained, a kennel offers your dog the comfort of dry living quarters, adequate ventilation and sunlight, and the availability of regular exercise.

Before you begin to draw up plans for kennel construction, check with your town's municipal offices to see if a building permit is required and which, if any, regulations of the building code you must adhere to. The permit, if required, must be obtained before any construction is begun. Building a kennel is not a small undertaking, so pre-planning on all fronts will prevent unexpected snags from cropping up, causing time delays and inconveniences.

One of the first decisions to make concerns the choice between building the kennel yourself as a sort of family project, or hiring a general contractor to do the work. If you decide on the latter, details of financing, building plans and blueprints to suit your needs should be worked out before contractual agreements are signed. For the plans on actual construction, including a concrete foundation, framework and overall structure, you should consult an architect who will, for a fee, draw up a set of blueprints for you or a contractor to follow. Have the architect see your land, and detail clearly to him each specific feature you want designed into the building. In this way you will enable him to set down a precise set of blueprints, meeting your specifications.

LAND AND SPACE REQUIREMENTS

To build an average size kennel, you must have a significant parcel of land to set aside for this purpose. The location of the building site should provide adequate sunlight and shade for warmth and coolness throughout the seasons. The soil should be of a high gravel content as a gravel soil provides good drainage. By comparison, a sandy soil, though its surface dries quickly, retains dampness and residual dirt just beneath the surface. It is also a favorite breeding place of fleas and similar pests.

Drainage is a prime consideration, not only to let natural ground water run off, but also to let the water drain off from the frequent hosings a kennel must be given to ensure cleanliness and prevent growth of disease-producing germs. A kennel should be trenched for drainage much the way a soldier trenches around his tent. One continuous drainage ditch approximately eight inches wide should be dug around all sides of the kennel, no further than a foot away from the kennel walls. It should be dug to a depth of four inches to start with, sloping an additional inch for every three yards of land. With ditches extending from at least two front corners of the building down to this surrounding ditch, water will run away from the building to the lowest point of land, preventing moisture build-up or preventing the water to lay near the kennel building itself. The drainage system can be sophisticated further, the ditch tiled, for instance, and eventually connecting with or running to a storm drain. Whatever else is devised, drainage should definitely figure into your building plans.

BUILDING MATERIALS

The building materials you use are of great importance. Not only must they be of good quality but they must be of a type that will protect the dog from the elements. For example, sheet metal, a conductor of both heat and cold, should never be used for the outside walls or ceilings. It becomes extremely hot in the sun and will retain heat in the kennel, making a potentially dangerous and certainly uncomfortable situation for the dogs. Outside walls should ideally be constructed from lumber, bricks or cinder blocks. The walls must be insulated with a substance that will serve equally well in all seasons, protecting your dogs from the heat and the cold.

Interior walls can be constructed of wood, plywood or plaster board. Plywood has the advantage of being extremely durable; however, plywood is quite expensive and can give way to splintering should the dogs scratch at it. Plaster board, also commonly known as sheet rock, is inexpensive and relatively durable. Plaster board does not, however, stand up well to moisture, but more than compensates for this drawback by being very resistant to insect and rodent infestation.

The above plans detail the probable steps involved in the construction of a rather large kennel, suited for up to a dozen dogs. At first, most dog owners have only one or two dogs that they want to provide for. If this is the case, a large dog house, modified somewhat, will aptly serve until such time that a larger kennel is needed.

THE SINGLE DOG HOUSE

While a dog will be contented with less living space than his master is accustomed to, his own house should be large enough to allow for free space around and above him when he stands up in the enclosure. The size of the dog house depends, of course, on the size of the dog.

Using materials purchased from any lumber store, you can build a dog house yourself. When constructing the house, take care to finish it off well, leaving no nails or wood splinters protruding from the wood which could injure the dog.

If you wish to move your pet into a new, ready-to-go home, finished dog houses can be purchased in varying styles and price ranges. Your pet shop may have some houses in stock; if not, the owner can probably suggest an outlet where one would be available. The yellow pages of your phone directory may also be useful in locating an establishment that carries dog houses, either constructed or in kits. Some of the latest styles available are quite pleasing to the eye, such as the house constructed out of unstripped logs, designed to give your dog his own little log cabin! If you check various outlets you will find that dog houses range in design from the simple to the elaborate.

CARE OF THE DOG HOUSE

To prevent dampness and to retain heat in the dog house, it should not be placed directly on the ground, but elevated at least several inches. A 2″ x 4″ beam placed under two opposing sides of the house, with the 4″ side lying flat on the ground, should allow for proper ventilation beneath the structure. However, in winter months you will want to close off this space to prevent drafts. In this case, boards can easily and quickly be nailed between the 2″ x 4″'s already in place to cover the exposed openings. Keeping the dog house a proper distance from the ground also serves to prevent the possibility of water damage, which will cause the wood to warp and eventually decay. Infestation of the wood by insects can be prevented by keeping the primary wood of the house from contact with the dirt below.

Whether kept in the yard or in the garage, the single dog house has the advantage of being able to be moved from spot to spot. Moving the dog house will be necessary occasionally for such reasons as cleaning, moving into or out of direct sunlight or shade, etc. This is an advantage when you consider that in the cold winter months your dog may very much appreciate having his house placed in direct sunlight! In cold weather the dog house can be positioned with the entranceway facing east or south, to receive full sunlight.

If a shifting of position is all that is needed, a strong friend or two should be able to help relocate the house. However, if the move is for a considerable distance and your dog house is quite heavy, a moving dolly may be necessary.

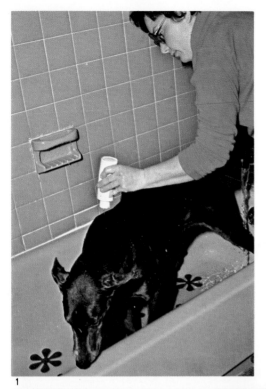

1

The Doberman Pinscher, because it is a short-haired breed, requires a minimum of grooming. Unlike many of the longer haired breeds, an occasional dry bath might suffice to keep him clean. When you do have to give him a "wet" bath it is not necessary to completely submerse to get him clean as pictures 1 through 4 indicate. 5) A young Doberman with his ears still taped from the cropping operation is put through a practice show stance.

2

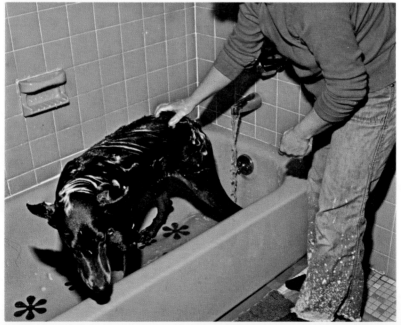

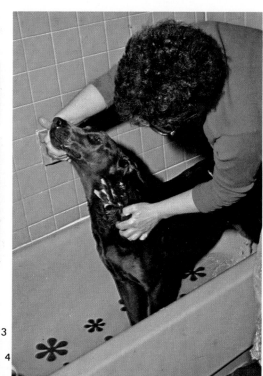

3

4

5

The Doberman Pinscher's physical prowess must match his mental capability if he is to master the feats of obedience competition and police and guard duties his working dog heritage put to him.

EXERCISE RUNS

If you want to let your dog out to exercise himself, yet do not care to fence in your entire property, wire runs are in order. The width of the runway should be at least a little more than the length of the dog; the length can be as long as the ground permits. The rule to follow is that any exercise run should be long enough to allow the dog to break into a short gallop. The runway grounds can be made of gravel, cement, or grass and natural ground. Cement and gravel runs provide quick drainage, whereas grass and dirt retain excrement and decayed food and become muddy with rain. If you choose to have natural runs, they must be dug and respaded twice a year. Many dog owners prefer to have cement foundations extend a few feet from the building, the rest of the run being grass. These short foundations can also be used as outdoor feeding places.

Large runs are generally constructed to a height of five to seven feet. To prevent the dogs from digging out under the fence, a trench eighteen inches deep can be dug and the fence placed inside. The bottom area is then filled with gravel and cement. Recover this area with dirt and pack it down tightly. This should thwart even the most determined digger!

11. DOBERMAN PINSCHERS AS WORKERS

From the earliest days of the breed, the Doberman Pinscher has always been intended to serve his master, whether it is in defending the home or helping to patrol the streets as a deterrent to crime. The continuous growth in popularity for the breed is evidence of the Dobe's ability to perform when it is most needed.

Police departments in both the United States and Europe have made good use of the Doberman's trainability in fighting crime. Before a Doberman is ever assigned to duty with a police force, he must undergo extensive training to assure that he is absolutely obedient to his master, for a life may hang in the balance. He must also be certified as being free from any physical or temperament impairments. Both dog and handler are taught to rely on each other as a team, to understand each other's patterns and to know exactly how to react in a given situation. Without these basic trusts, a police team cannot perform their duties fearlessly and unhesitantly.

In large cities Doberman Pinschers are frequently used by policemen on their normal street rounds. If the patrolman should find some evidence of a forced entry to a building, he will often release his Doberman partner to search for any possible intruders. The Dobe makes good use of his keen senses and can generally locate and subdue any hidden criminal. If necessary, he will take them by force, but he is trained to corner and hold them at bay until released by his master. Another function of the police-trained Doberman Pinscher is to serve as a crime-prevention tool. The sight of a Doberman is generally enough to ensure adequate crowd control in congested areas, and police forces are recording great success in using Doberman patrols in large parks or recreational areas that were once centers for muggings and other crime.

THE DOBERMAN AND MILITARY SERVICE

Archeological evidence surviving from Roman, Greek and Persian civilizations shows that dogs have been used for military purposes for thousands of years. In modern times the courage and fortitude of the Doberman Pinscher breed has been utilized in association with police and war work, in the course of which they have been called upon in life and death situations to attack and defend their charge.

The British have used the Doberman extensively as a rescuer and on guard post duty. By the beginning of World War I Germany employed thousands of Dobermans and German Shepherd Dogs in war service.

1) One of this Dobe kennel owner's dogs keeps a close watch while she cleans an individual pen. In a large kennel concrete flooring on the runs is most practical for purposes of sanitation. 2) A young Doberman waits expectantly for his daily run. 3) A large kennel picturing occupants' individual runs and indoor shelter shared by all occupants in common. 4) Straw and other similar types of materials are strewn on the floor of outside runs to help absorb droppings. Here the kennel owner rakes out used straw before replacing it with clean absorbent material.

3

4

The skills a dog is required to master to earn CD, CDX, and UD certificates are a logical departure point for entry into the Schutzhund trials, which complete his training to a fine level of skill for police work and related fields.

The Doberman was used chiefly in surveying the battlefield in search of wounded soldiers. Upon discovering a man stranded on the battlefield they would return to camp to alert others, leading them back to aid the wounded soldier. Seeking out enemy strongholds was another of these remarkable dogs' functions, and they were so efficient that they were included in the U.S. Marine landing fleet in the assault on the South Pacific in World War II.

12. SCHUTZHUND COMPETITION

Recognized world-wide, Schutzhund degrees signify the most advanced performance of skills and training achieved in obedience competition. Originated in Europe by the German Working Dog Association (DVG), Schutzhund trials were one of a number of competitive tests designed to determine the highest level possible at which a dog could perform as a true working dog. Designed into these tests was the capacity to evaluate the dog's temperament, his courage, protective instincts, fighting drive, responsiveness, and eagerness to please. For the duties for which the dog was earmarked it was necessary for him to work amicably yet efficiently with humans and to have an overall moderate behavior pattern. These tests were used as a basis on which to build controlled breeding programs that would keep the high quality of·the dog and its original purpose free from corruption.

The North American Working Dog Association (NASA), the American equivalent of the DVG, sets the standards for all training and approving of Schutzhund trials. It views the trials and the fine degree of training they give rise to as a sport, the outcome of which is a highly trained dog, *not* an attack dog but one capable of performing at peak efficiency in interaction with his human companion. The NASA views the Schutzhund trials as an extension of the familiar CD, CDX, UD, and TD titles, and in fact encourages the Dobe owner aspiring to the Schutzhund (SchH) titles to earn these on his way, as they fully cover two-thirds of the requirements necessary to obtain the SchH degrees.

The SchH trials are broken down into four levels of skills for which a degree can be achieved. They are SchH A, SchH I, SchH II, and SchH III and progress in difficulty of feats to be accomplished in that order. Contenders for these titles must successfully accomplish the requirements demanded by one level before they are allowed to compete on the next level. In general, the skills that must be performed on each level are similar, but become more complex, demanding more discreet actions per overall routine or operation as the dog progresses from one level to the next.

The first trial, Schutzhund A, is practically identical to Schutzhund I except that it leaves out the tracking exercise required by the latter. It is equivalent to the beginner's exercise and is comprised of two sections, Obedience and Protection, each of which may achieve a score of 100 points. The Obedience phase of this trial covers most of the fundamental exercises performed in the Companion Dog and Utility Dog competi-

1) A red Dobe sits during an outdoor training session. 2) Trainer begins teaching the "come" command to a young Doberman.

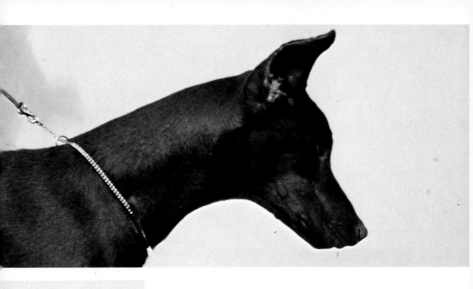

1) Profile of Doberman shows choke collar used during training sessions. 2) A beautifully trained adult Dobe demonstrates the "sit-stay" while his master walks away from him. 3) Heavy canvas training harness of the type appropriate for large dogs.

2

3

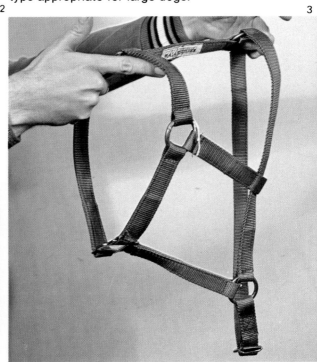

tions, except that in the Schutzhund test the dog must demonstrate his ability to withstand the sound of gunfire while off lead. Shying at this point means failure of the test.

In the Protection part of SchH A, the dog must prove his ability to interact as a deterrent with a human decoy who plays the part of an assailant or aggressor against his master or close associates. On this level, the types of actions required from the dog are fairly simple in the overall context of the SchH trials, requiring, among others, that the dog seek out the person posing as the criminal and alert his handler to the decoy's position without showing any further aggression toward him.

SchH I is identical with the Protection portions of SchH II and SchH III except the demands made upon the dog's combative skill are increased with each level. He must, for instance, ward off attacks on himself with sticks, and attacks upon his handler. In SchH III he must even deal with two combatants instead of one.

In the Tracking phase of the trials, the dog must follow an unmarked trail that is not immediately fresh, finding and retrieving a specific number of articles. With each succeeding trial level, the length of the trail, the time elapsed since it was laid, and the number of articles the dog is required to seek out and retrieve, increase.

The Obedience section resembles that of the Companion and Utility Dog events, as has already been stated, with the exercises the dog is required to do increasing in number, length of times the dog must remain on stay, height of hurdles to be jumped, and weight of objects he is required to retrieve.

More degrees than just the Schutzhund titles may be awarded at the NASA sanctioned SchH trials. Examinations are also held for the AD Endurance Test; FH or Advanced Tracking Dog; INT, the International Degree; and PD I and PD II awards for Police Dog test. As at the Schutzhund Dog trials, a licensed judge officiates and is authorized to award degrees in the tests as well as in the SchH trials.

Before a dog may compete for the Schutzhund titles, he must be at least 14 months old. No Doberman is permitted to be a serious contender for any of these degrees until he has passed a temperament test, proving that he is temperamentally stable. Orientation to these tests, their structure and field environment can begin when a puppy is just three months old; serious training should not be begun until a dog is at least nine months old.

While the Schutzhund trials were originally set up in Europe to ascertain the quality of any or all working dogs, the Doberman Pinscher in particular has made a name for itself in this area. More than likely it is because Herr Louis Dobermann's original intent for this dog, bred to be

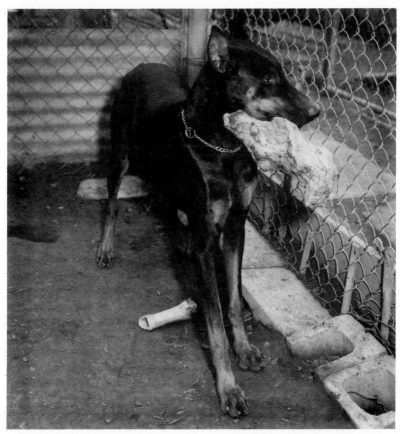

The healthy Dobe, kept in its prime through good diet, regular exercise and a disciplined schedule of training, will retain his playful nature and youthful attitude for a longer time than one allowed to become soft through inactivity and too many treats.

a working dog of lean yet powerful stature and to serve its human companions closely in critical areas of protective function, is well served by the activities and mental keenness demanded in the Schutzhund trials. The abilities and instincts bred into the Doberman are tested to the limit in these trials and individuals of the breed have the opportunity to show their real mettle. Seeing their dogs in action enables handlers and breeders to determine those that should be used as the foundation of future breeding programs aimed at maintaining the very highest standards for the breed.